Critical Guides to Spanish Texts

26 García Lorca: Bodas de sangre

Critical Guides to Spanish Texts

EDITED BY JOHN VAREY, ALAN DEYERMOND, & CATHERINE DAVIES

GARCÍA LORCA

BODAS DE SANGRE

C.B. Morris

Professor of Spanish
University of California, Los Angeles

Grant & Cutler Ltd
1996

© Grant & Cutler Ltd 1996

ISBN 0 7293 0083 8

First edition 1980
Reprinted, with a revised bibliography 1996

DEPÓSITO LEGAL: V. 4.936 - 1995

Printed in Spain by
Gráficas Soler, S.A., Valencia
for
GRANT & CUTLER LTD
55–57 GREAT MARLBOROUGH STREET, LONDON W1V 2AY

Contents

Prefatory note

QUOTATIONS from Lorca's works are taken from the twentieth edition of the two-volume *Obras completas* (Madrid: Aguilar, 1977). Quotations from *Bodas de sangre* are accompanied by a reference to the act and scene; all other quotations will be accompanied by a volume and page number. The figures in parentheses in italic type refer to the numbered items in the Bibliographical Note; where necessary these are followed by page numbers.

1. *"Sour misfortune's book"*

> ROMEO: O give me thy hand,
> One writ with me in sour misfortune's book!
>
> Shakespeare, *The Tragedy of Romeo and Juliet*

IT is at times difficult to distinguish between Lorca the poet and Lorca the dramatist; to read a gypsy ballad such as the 'Romance del emplazado' is to witness a poet's rich inventiveness shaped and controlled by a dramatist's instinct for perspective and changes of pace and setting. Similarly, the poetic texture of what many characters in his plays say and sing is an integral and indispensable feature of his dramatic craftsmanship. This fusion of poetry and the theatre was both an instinctive practice and a deliberate policy, which he carefully pursued and constantly expounded in the 1930s. In his interview with Felipe Morales in 1936 he defined the theatre as 'poetry that rises out of a book and becomes human'. The dramatic characters he created make it clear that the poetry they embodied was for him a poetry of elegy and lament; his placing of characters on a plane above reality responded to a painful awareness of human suffering, apparent in his choice of the verbs 'shout', 'weep' and 'despair':

> El teatro es la poesía que se levanta del libro y se hace humana. Y al hacerse habla y grita, llora y se desespera. El teatro necesita que los personajes que aparezcan en la escena lleven un traje de poesía y al mismo tiempo que se les vean los huesos, la sangre. (II, p. 1078)

If drama is poetry that becomes human, it follows that a poet is the person best qualified and uniquely gifted to write it.

With an assurance uncramped by false modesty, Lorca declared
unequivocally in another interview — the one he gave to Nicolás González-Deleito in 1935 — that "El teatro que ha per-
durado siempre es el de los poetas" (II, p. 1046). His generous
tributes in the same interview to Carlos Arniches and José
Zorrilla — two dramatists who in no way match the depth,
quality or vision of Lorca — were directed towards the 'fantasy'
of the first and the 'poetic atmosphere' of the second. *Bodas
de sangre* is rich in both; on the other hand, many plays, Lorca
states in a graphic image not devoid of arrogance, lie enfolded
in their shrouds because they were written in verse:

> El teatro que ha perdurado siempre es el de los poetas.
> Siempre ha estado el teatro en manos de los poetas. Y ha
> sido mejor el teatro en tanto era más grande el poeta. No
> es —claro— el poeta lírico, sino el poeta dramático.... La
> gente está acostumbrada al teatro poético en verso. Si el
> autor es un versificador, no ya un poeta, el público le
> guarda cierto respeto. Tiene respeto al verso en teatro.
> El verso no quiere decir poesía en el teatro. Don Carlos
> Arniches es más poeta que casi todos los que escriben
> teatro en verso actualmente. No puede haber teatro sin
> ambiente poético, sin invención... Fantasía hay en el
> sainete más pequeño de don Carlos Arniches... La obra
> de éxito más perdurable ha sido la de un poeta, y hay
> mil obras escritas en versos muy bien escritos que están
> amortajadas en sus fosas.... Teatro poético, teatro román-
> tico, el de Zorrilla. (II, p. 1046)

With all the confidence and insight which success and self-
knowledge can bring, Lorca established a series of precise contrasts in this statement: between "teatro poético en verso" and
"teatro poético"; between "verso" — or "versos muy bien es-
critos" — and "poesía"; between a "versificador" and a "poeta" — or, to use his exact term, a "poeta dramático". He had no
doubts about what to call himself; so much is evident from
his announcement under the cast list of *La casa de Bernarda
Alba*: "El poeta advierte que estos tres actos tienen la inten-
ción de un documental fotográfico." Nor did he have any mis-
givings about the poetic elements of his plays in general and

of *Bodas de sangre* in particular; when Pedro Massa asked him in 1933: "¿Qué momento le satisface más en *Bodas de sangre*, Federico?", he replied unhesitatingly:

> Aquel en que intervienen la Luna y la Muerte, como elementos y símbolos de la fatalidad. El realismo que preside hasta ese instante la tragedia se quiebra y desaparece para dar paso a la fantasía poética, donde es natural que yo me encuentre como el pez en el agua. (II, p. 959)

It was those symbolic figures, clad unmistakably in their "traje de poesía", who disconcerted some of the critics who saw the first performance of *Bodas de sangre* in the Teatro Beatriz, Madrid, on 8th March, 1933. Those who faulted the play for "ciertos vicios de colorismo barroco" and its author for "llevarse a exageración el recurso del símbolo poético" [1] were insensitive to the fact that poetry — in the form of images, songs, symbols and symbolic characters — is essential to the fabric and purpose of Lorca's first tragedy. The quality of the poetry in *Bodas de sangre* and the way in which Lorca wove it inextricably into its texture are thrown into relief by setting the tragedy against the plays of Arniches and Zorrilla, whom he mentioned admiringly, and of Antonio and Manuel Machado, who belong to the unnamed group "que escriben teatro en verso actualmente". The "fantasía" and "invención" he praised in Arniches are to be found in the multiplicity of characters, who, ranging from doctors to shop assistants, move in settings as varied as "el interior de un lavadero cubierto" in *El chico de las peñuelas* (1915), and "el patio de un establecimiento de coches de alquiler" in *El señor Adrián el primo* (1927). Arniches's skill at making people reveal themselves by the way they speak is shown by Doctor Izquierdo's pretentious diagnosis in *La locura de Don Juan* (1923): "Era un caso igual al tuyo, exactamente igual... abulia, astenia volitiva, falta de energía, de voluntad...", and by Sisinio's lighthearted topical song in *El último mono* (1926): "Charlestón, Charlestón, es el

---

[1] Anon., 'La semana teatral', *Sparta. Revista de espectáculos* [Madrid], Año II, no. 20, 18th March, 1933; A. C., 'Beatriz: *Bodas de sangre*', *ABC*, 9th March, 1933.

baile que Charlot bailó en Boston..." [2] This ability to match speech to character was not lost on Lorca, who displayed his skill at devising natural and finely attuned dialogue in the exchanges between Leonardo and the Suegra in Act I, scene ii, and between the Madre and Padre in Act I, scene iii.

In declaring that the plays they wrote jointly were written "en verso", Antonio and Manuel Machado acknowledged the difference between verse and poetry to which Lorca also drew attention; that difference is highlighted by José Luis's contempt in *La Lola se va a los puertos* (1929) for "Esos gansos / que desprecian cuanto ignoran", which is a limp and graceless echo, bordering on parody, of Antonio Machado's trenchant indictment in *Campos de Castilla*:

> Castilla miserable, ayer dominadora,
> envuelta en sus andrajos desprecia cuanto ignora.

When in the same play Heredia is made to say:

> todo se americaniza,
> se desustancia...,

it is clear that in writing plays in verse the Machado brothers did not pursue as ideals euphony and verbal elegance. When Lorca made the Novia declare to the Madre: "Yo era una mujer quemada, llena de llagas por dentro y por fuera..." (III, ii), he described her fevered mind and body in a graphic image reminiscent of the wounds of Christ; he did not need to resort to the awkward diction used by Araceli in *Las adelfas* (1928), whose pretentious, staccato speech is a good example of its authors' clumsy, tuneless verse:

> Charlatanes, embusteros...
> Hidroterapía: con agua
> se sana de todo: helio-
> terapía: donde entre el sol
> hace milagros; los nervios

---

[2] Arniches, *La locura de Don Juan, El Teatro*, Año II, no. 23, 6th March, 1926, p. 24: *El último mono, o el chico de la tienda, El Teatro Moderno*, Año II, no. 69, 1st January, 1927, p. 39.

se entonan con nerviosina,
el nombre es casi un remedio;
homeopatía: un granito
de anís y te pones nuevo...[3]

The broken rhythm of this speech contrasts with the flow of Zorrilla's well-lubricated, confident lines, exemplified by Don Juan's protestation of love to Doña Inés in Act IV, scene iii of *Don Juan Tenorio*:

No; el amor que hoy se atesora
en mi corazón mortal,
no es un amor terrenal
como el que sentí hasta ahora;
no es esa chispa fugaz
que cualquier ráfaga apaga;
es incendio que se traga
cuanto ve, inmenso, voraz.[4]

The same traditional image of the fire of love reappears in the Novia's self-justification to the Madre, but whereas Don Juan's words, in spite of the clockwork rhymes which regulate them, give the impression of prose, the Novia's words — with their diverse and interwoven images of cold, frost, water, birds, hobbling, withering and burning — possess a dense metaphoric texture which marks them as the work of a gifted and sensitive *poeta dramático*:

Y yo corría con tu hijo que era como un niño de agua fría y el otro me mandaba cientos de pájaros que me impedían el andar y que dejaban escarcha sobre mis heridas de pobre mujer marchita, de muchacha acariciada por el fuego. (III, ii)

[3] Manuel and Antonio Machado, *Obras completas*, ed. Heliodoro Carpintero (Madrid: Plenitud, 1962), pp. 735, 481, 417.
[4] Zorrilla, *Don Juan Tenorio* (Barcelona: Labor, 1975), pp. 162-3. J. M. Aguirre has postulated Zorrilla's influence on Lorca in 'Zorrilla y García Lorca: leyendas y romances gitanos', *Bulletin Hispanique*, LXXXI (1979), 75-92.

The essential difference between Lorca on the one hand and Zorrilla and the Machado brothers on the other is that in Lorca, on the evidence of the Novia's speech alone, every word counts. The dense verbal texture of *Bodas de sangre* demonstrates that Lorca devoted limitless care and deep thought to devising patterns of imagery, multiple echoes and levels of meaning which invite the reader to connect the horse of fact with the horse of fantasy, the knife of murderous reality with the knife-like moonbeams. It comes as no surprise to learn that he spent five years pondering over *Bodas de sangre* before writing it in a few weeks; he made that and other fascinating observations about his methods of work to Nicolás González-Deleito:

> En escribir tardo mucho. Me paso tres y cuatro años pensando una obra de teatro y luego la escribo en quince días.... Cinco años tardé en hacer *Bodas de sangre;* tres invertí en *Yerma...* De la realidad son fruto las dos obras. Reales son sus figuras; rigurosamente auténtico el tema de cada una de ellas... Primero, notas, observaciones tomadas de la vida misma, del periódico a veces... Luego, un pensar en torno al asunto. Un pensar largo, constante, enjundioso. (II, p. 1047)

Five years take us back to 1928, the year in which he found the title and the actual events which, embroidered by newspaper reporters hungry for sensations, provoked the 'long, constant, deep thought' that was to ripen into his first tragedy. *Bodas de sangre* represents no new departure, follows no new direction in Lorca's career; rather is it an elaboration of moods, themes and personal convictions which dominated the poems and plays he wrote during those five years of reflexion. What he did and saw and felt during that period shaped and coloured the events he read in the newspapers as well as the diverse literary and folkloric reminiscences which complemented and enriched them. His visit to New York in 1929-30 aggravated rather than relieved the emotional and spiritual troubles from which he was trying to escape, and all that he witnessed in New York — like the six suicides in one day he mentioned to Pablo Suero in 1933 (II, p. 978) — deepened his consciousness of death, human misery and the frailty of the body. In the poems of *Poeta en Nueva York* many creatures are killed or mutilated with a hideous arsenal of weapons, among them the knives that will be wielded murderously in *Bodas de sangre*. In the Madre's closing words — her dirge to the "cuchillito" — Lorca repeated his frightening evocation of a scream triggered by a knife's passage through flesh, which is an essential part of the miniature drama enacted in his poem 'Asesinato (Dos vóces de madrugada en Riverside Drive)':

> —*¿Cómo fue?*
> —Una grieta en la mejilla.
> ¡Eso es todo!
> Una uña que aprieta el tallo.
> Un alfiler que bucea
> hasta encontrar las raicillas del grito.
> Y el mar deja de moverse.
> —*¿Cómo, cómo fue?*
> —Así.
> —*¡Déjame! ¿De esa manera?*
> —Sí.
> El corazón salió solo.
> —*¡Ay, ay de mí!* (I, p. 477)

The poem 'Danza de la muerte', as it takes our minds back in time towards the medieval *danse macabre,* hymns the triumphant timelessness of death, which will claim in *Bodas de sangre* both the wrongdoer, Leonardo, and the man he wronged, the Novio. The conviction Lorca voiced in *Poeta en Nueva York* that "la vida no es buena, ni noble, ni sagrada" (I, p. 530) clearly extends into and overlaps onto *Bodas de sangre.* So do the themes of the plays he wrote between 1928 and 1933, particularly those of *La zapatera prodigiosa* (1930) and *Amor de don Perlimplín con Belisa en su jardín* (1931), which are linked thematically by the incompatibility of man and wife. In the first play it is clear that the shoemaker's departure and the allegorical puppet-show he gives in disguise have achieved nothing; and with his suicide Perlimplín sacrifices himself to Belisa's heated desires and feverish illusions, which he knew he could never satisfy. The interweaving of love and death in this play, despite Lorca's tragicomic treatment, foreshadows *Bodas de sangre* and hearkens back to Romeo and Juliet, whose love runs as a connecting thread through *El público* (1933).

In *Bodas de sangre* Lorca knew what he wanted to say and how he wanted to say it, and the suspicion that he did not know how to resolve the love felt by the shoemaker and by Perlimplín for their younger wives must give way to admiration for the way in which in his first tragedy Lorca moulded and manipulated his characters, be they human or unearthly. La Luna and La Mendiga are merely symbolic representations of the death that is so essential a part of the Madre's thoughts and emotions; they should offer none of the surprise provoked by the presence of a Jugador de Rugby in *Así que pasen cinco años* (1931); they fit naturally into a play that explores and dramatizes the force of passionate feelings and their relationship with death. The apparent inseparability of passion and death explains why Lorca's mind was engaged by the title of a film shown in Spain in 1928, *Bodas sangrientas*, and by events reported in newspapers in July of the same year. With the film he made in 1973, *Les Noces rouges*, Claude Chabrol showed the durable appeal of a title involving blood and marriage. Based on Luciano Doria's novel *Beatriz Cenci*, *Bodas sangrientas* has a plot so labyrinthine that it defies comparison with the sparse lines and direct movement of Lorca's tragedy. However, Lorca's acquaintance with the film is suggested not merely by his own title, whose similarity is striking, but by his dramatization of the powerful emotional conflicts which are so essential a part of the film: between deep, secret love and hatred; between vengeance and self-sacrifice. According to the melodramatic, exuberant prose summary of the film, the Duque Mario Savelli "profesaba una pasión intensa y arrolladora a Beatriz" and felt for her husband "un odio devastador y tempestuoso". [5] Real-life characters were prey to equally intense passions in Almería in July 1928.

On 24th July, 1928 the *Heraldo de Madrid* carried a story of elopement and murder under this triple headline: "Miste-

---

[5] *Bodas sangrientas. Grandioso drama histórico de la PITTALUGA FILM*, Las Selecciones Gaumont "Diamante Azul" (Barcelona, n.d.).

rioso crimen en un cortijo de Níjar / Momentos antes de veri-
ficarse la boda se fuga con un primo para burlar al novio /
Les sale al encuentro un enmascarado y mata a tiros al raptor."
Sequels appeared daily until 28th July elaborating on the flight
of Francisca Cañada Morales with her cousin Francisco (Curro)
Montes Cañada moments before her marriage to Casimiro Pérez Pino; the whole train of circumstances set in motion by
the elopement was summarized on 30th July in a headline that
anticipated the writing of *Bodas de sangre*: "Epílogo de un
crimen de romance andaluz / El rapto de Frasquita por Curro
Montes ha originado una muerte, un caso de locura, otro de
enfermedad grave, el dolor de tres familias y... bastante literatura." There are enough coincidences between *Bodas de sangre* and these reports in the *Heraldo de Madrid* to show that
Lorca was so intrigued by the event and the circumstances
surrounding it that he remembered and embroidered a number
of details, particularly those relating to Curro Montes, the model
for his Leonardo. Like Leonardo, Curro Montes owned a horse
and "montaba habitualmente" (27th July); and it was on his
horse that he and his cousin escaped while the guests celebrated
the wedding (26th July). According to the imaginative report
published on 26th July, the elopement was proposed by Curro
Montes after reproaching his cousin with a series of rebukes
and sneers about money which Lorca was to echo when he set
Leonardo and the Novia face to face before her wedding:

 —Conque te casas ¿eh? —le dijo a modo de reproche.
 —Sí; ¿qué quieres? Me caso —contestaría ella, sin
poner, seguramente, mucho fuego, y sí antes alguna tris-
teza resignada, en sus palabras.
 —Tú no te casas con ese hombre. No quiero yo. No
quieres tú tampoco. Lo estoy leyendo en tus ojos. Casimiro no puede hacerte feliz porque... porque no, porque no te gusta.
 —Pero es bueno, es honrado, es trabajador, y me
quiere.
 —Lo que quiere es el dinero de tu padre. ¿Cómo
te voy a dejar yo que te cases con él, si veo que no le
quieres, que me sigues queriendo a mí? ¿Recuerdas?

Although she had been engaged to Casimiro for two years, Francisca — like Lorca's Novia — was in love not with him but with Curro (25th July), whose impulsiveness and dynamism proved more exciting and electric than the placidity of her fiancé, "tímido y callado" according to one report (27th July) and idealized in another as an "Hombre de buen carácter, modesto, sencillo" (26th July). Francisca's description of Curro as "enamorado" (28th July) and the reporter's comment that the latter "era muy mujeriego y tenía una novia en cada cortijada" (30th July) offered Lorca an example of sexual magnetism which he was to reproduce in Leonardo and echo in his widow's eulogy:

> Era hermoso jinete
> y ahora montón de nieve.
> Corrió ferias y montes
> y brazos de mujeres. (III, ii)

Intriguing as these similarities are, their existence poses two questions: why should Lorca the man remember the event which inspired them, and what did he as a dramatist make out of it? The answers to these questions are related. In the first place, the event and its repercussions demonstrated to him a painful fact of life: that an impulsive action, a human error, can enmesh guilty and innocent alike in a network of sorrowful consequences. At the end of *Bodas de sangre* the Novia's father is dishonoured, Leonardo's wife is wronged and widowed and his children — one unborn — are fatherless; they are blameless victims of an irreversible sequence of circumstances foreshadowed in the happenings at Níjar and summarized in the *Heraldo de Madrid* on 30th July:

> A estas horas, por culpa de Frasquita, hay un hombre procesado, perdido por haber dado muerte a otro hombre; hay una vida segada en flor, la de Curro Montes; una mujer, la hermana de la víctima (de la principal víctima, porque, en realidad, no ha habido una sola), atacada de locura subitánea, efecto de la tremenda impresión recibida al saber la trágica muerte de su hermano; una mujer y sus hijos, abandonados, sin padre; un honrado

trabajador, Casimiro, que ante las burlas de que es objeto después del trance grotesco en que le colocó la veleidad de su prometida ha resuelto poner tierra de por medio y buscar el modo de rehacer su vida bajo otros cielos más amparadores, para huir del ludibrio que le rodea en la provincia de Almería. Hay, finalmente, un anciano, el padre de Frasquita, en quien convergen y se resumen todos los dolores sembrados por los desatentados amores de Frasquita con su primo Curro Montes.

Lorca himself answered the second question — what did he as a dramatist make out of the event? — in his insistence when interviewed by Juan Chabás in 1934 that "Hay que volver a la tragedia" (II, p. 1027), for it was that real-life interlocking of destinies that was to inspire his tragic interpretation of circumstances in *Bodas de sangre*. The same tragic vision coloured his choice of the literary and other reminiscences which he inserted into his play, and explains why the common denominator of so many of them is misfortune and foreboding. One of the most striking features of *Bodas de sangre* is Lorca's harmonious fusing of elements which he derived from his wide reading and from that rich fund of popular lore which in its very irrationality complements the irrational urges felt by the most impulsive characters in the play. The "sinrazón" lamented by the Novia in the forest (III, i) refers both to what people do and to what people think, and it is Lorca's sensitive perception of people's thoughts and feelings that makes their superstitious beliefs blend naturally into a tragedy dealing with passions that defy reason and social decorum. When he personified the moon in the final act as "un leñador joven con la cara blanca" (III, i), he was able to connect it with the Leñadores by capitalizing dramatically on the popular and universal beliefs that the moon is "un desgraciado leñador que yendo caminando para su casa una noche a tiempo que salía la luna, la hizo burla y la luna se lo tragó". In the same scene the coincidence of La Luna, La Mendiga and the *cerco* of men surrounding the lovers is an enactment of the superstition that "Cerco en la luna anuncia lluvia o desgracias," a superstition recorded in a *copla* which Lorca could well have put into the Novia's mouth:

Cerco tiene la luna,
mi amante es muerto;
no miro para ella
~ de sentimiento.

Similarly, when the Muchacha 2.ᵃ wants the Novia to confirm
after her wedding that "los dos alfileres sirven para casarse,
¿verdad?" (II, ii), she voices the common belief that "La moza
soltera a quien una recién casada dé uno de los alfileres que
lleva prendidos el día de la boda al desnudarse, se casará dentro
del año". [6] However, when the Novia deflates the girl's eager-
ness to marry with the dispirited rejoinder "¿Para qué?", she
questions not the belief but marriage itself.

However innocent they may seem, these folkloric elements
are as ominous in a play entitled *Bodas de sangre* as the recurrence of the number three. That number seems to have held
some fear for Lorca; Pablo Suero has recounted that "nos
reímos todos de la superstición de gitanos" when Lorca —
"asustado" — refused with the categoric shout "¡Tres, no!" to
be one of three people whose cigarettes were to be lit by the
same match (II, p. 984). Modelled on the Greek Fates, the two
Muchachas and the Niña who appear in the final scene remind
us with their poetic commentary that for all of us the cutting
of the thread of life is the third and final stage in the triple
division of our stay on earth into birth, life and death. Preceded
by the three woodcutters and succeeded by the three mourning
widows, these three Fates, whom Lorca naturalized into a Spanish country setting, are the central trio in the three groups of
figures whose presence in the final act complements visually
the recurrence of the number three in the first act; just as the
death in the distant past of her husband led the Madre to
bewail "tres años escasos" and "Los tres años que estuvo casado conmigo" (I, iii), so will the imminent death of Leonardo
and the Novio give lethal point to the remarks, made by the
Novio and the Suegra (I, i and I, ii), that Leonardo and the
Novia were engaged for three years. The lives and destinies

---

[6] Antonio Machado y Álvarez, *Biblioteca de las tradiciones populares españolas* (Madrid: Fe, 1884-6), VIII, p. 266; I, p. 215; VIII,
p. 270.

of the Novio and Leonardo are further intertwined when the Madre promises to buy her son three suits for his wedding (I, i) and when the Criada tells the Novia she heard a horse — quickly identified as the one ridden by Leonardo — "A las tres" (I, iii).

Other elements of *Bodas de sangre* show that Lorca had an eye for details, particularly when they contained a visually ominous quality. Leonardo's horse — "reventando de sudor", according to his wife (I, ii) — hints at frenzied rides as graphically as the horses "llenos de polvo y de sudor" led by Don Alvaro's negro slave in the first act of Rivas's play (I, iv). The gesture made by an old woman in the second *jornada* (scene 4) of Valle-Inclán's *Águila de blasón* (1907) clearly appealed to Lorca; when his Mendiga, at the end of the forest scene, "Abre el manto y queda en el centro como un gran pájaro de alas inmensas" (III, i), she spreads herself like a bird in the sinister way adopted by Valle-Inclán's *vieja*:

> Vuelan los gorriones en bandadas, y en lo alto de la higuera abre los brazos el espantajo grotesco de una vieja vestida de harapos... [7]

The recognition of such details is less important than sensing the tragic complexion which Lorca gave them. The tragic vision of *Bodas de sangre* has intrigued a number of critics. For Reed Anderson, the tragedy of this play lies in the defeat or reversal of the principles "by which people are either bound or brought into relationships with one another"; consequently, for this critic, "The over-all view is of a society violently divided, with family units mutilated and emotions distorted by the antagonisms that prevail in social life" (*3*, pp. 175, 186). Another critic, Luis González del Valle, has tried unconvincingly to interpret the play in Aristotelian terms, arriving at the limp conclusion that "lo trágico" in *Bodas de sangre* lies in "la soledad de la Novia" and in "la desaparición de toda esperanza de continuación de la estirpe" (*9*, p. 108). Unexceptionable as their views may be, they suffer from being made in a literary vac-

---

[7] *Águila de blasón*, 2nd ed. (Madrid: Austral, 1964), p. 41.

uum: the tragic vision which inspires the play is highlighted
by connecting it with the tragedies of Lope de Vega, John
Millington Synge and Shakespeare. Jean J. Smoot has established between Synge's *Riders to the Sea* and *Bodas de sangre*
a number of connexions, whose presence reflects Lorca's reading of the play with his friend Miguel Cerón in 1920 or 1921
and his acquaintance with Juan Ramón Jiménez's translation
of it. As Smoot insists, the Madre is as obsessed with death
as Synge's Maurya; and in both plays death is both the dom-
inant theme and a menacing presence which pursues men and
motivates a scene of women kneeling.

Ernesto Jareño has postulated a number of coincidences
between Lorca's tragedy and Lope de Vega's *El caballero de
Olmedo:* the dramatization of an actual event; the intervention
of symbolic characters, like the Labrador and Sombra in Lope's
play; and the murder at night (*12*, pp. 221-2). As *El caballero
de Olmedo* belonged to the repertoire of La Barraca, Lorca
obviously knew the play well; Jareño also suggests that he
knew *A Midsummer Night's Dream* and *The Tragedy of Romeo
and Juliet.* The *prestidigitador*'s allusion to the first play in the
sixth *cuadro* of *El público* (II, p. 528) suggests a familiarity
which is reinforced by the forest setting: Shakespeare's "haunted grove" (III, ii) — the situation for "the fierce vexation of
a dream" (IV, i) — is as remote from reality as Lorca's forest,
where sounds, characters, events and lighting effects relate it
to the magic or forbidden forests of folk literature. When Lorca
tried to define the urge to create a poem, he used an image
reminiscent of tales about treasure forests and hunting in forbidden forests; in his lecture 'La imagen poética de Don Luis
de Góngora' (1927) he declared that

> El poeta que va a hacer un poema (lo sé por experien-
> cia propia) tiene la sensación vaga de que va a una
> cacería nocturna en un bosque lejanísimo. Un miedo
> inexplicable rumorea en el corazón. (I, pp. 1013-14)

A comparison between *Bodas de sangre* and *The Tragedy
of Romeo and Juliet* is much more fruitful, because it demonstrates that the tragic interpretation Lorca gave to similar cir-

cumstances sets his play fully in a context and tradition of tragedy. Several references in his works show that Shakespeare's lovers and their passion haunted him; in his article 'Historia de este gallo' (1928) *Romeo y Julieta* stands out from the melodramatic *El suspiro del moro* and the ludicrous *Vaso de agua* as favourite titles proposed by three speakers (I, p. 1158). A similar contrast sets the two lovers apart from violence in *Poema del cante jondo* (1920), where in the 'Escena del teniente coronel de la Guardia Civil' Lorca imagined the following stage direction:

> (Romeo y Julieta, celeste, blanco y oro, se abrazan sobre el jardín de tabaco de la caja de puros. El militar acaricia el cañón de un fusil lleno de sombra submarina.)
> (I, p. 226)

In 1930 the relief he felt at escaping to Cuba from the horrors of New York again put him in mind of Shakespeare's lovers:

> Y con el rosal de Romeo y Julieta.
> Iré a Santiago. (I, p. 541)

The fourth Estudiante's recollection in the fifth *cuadro* of *El público* that "El tumulto comenzó cuando vieron que Romeo y Julieta se amaban de verdad" (II, p. 516) could also be applied to the events that follow the elopement of Leonardo and the Novia. Their flight on horseback to the dark forest and its association in Lorca's mind with the fate of Romeo and Juliet are indicated by the invitation made by the Caballo Blanco 1 to Juliet to mount him and ride "A lo oscuro":

CABALLO BLANCO 1
Monta en mi grupa.

JULIETA
¿Para qué?

CABALLO BLANCO 1 *(Acercándose.)*
Para llevarte.

JULIETA

¿Dónde?

CABALLO BLANCO 1

A lo oscuro. En lo oscuro hay ramas suaves. El ce-
menterio de las alas tiene mil superficies de espesor.
(II, p. 493)

The words which Lorca scribbled on the manuscript of *El público* — "(aquí las palabras del drama Shamspear)" [8] — suggest
that his knowledge of Shakespeare's tragedy went further than
the names of the lovers and respect for their proverbial love.
A first and strong point of contact between the two plays is
the family feuds, whose lethal durability ensures in both tragedies the bloody interplay of love and hate mourned by Juliet:

My only love, sprung from my only hate!
Too early seen unknown, and known too late!
Prodigious birth of love it is to me
That I must love a loathèd enemy. (I, v)

Juliet's impossible love for Romeo blinds her to the virtues of
Paris, who — in Capulet's words — "Stuffed, as they say, with
honourable parts" (III, v), is idealized as systematically as the
Novio. Romeo, undeterred like Leonardo by "stony limits" and
victim like him of "some distemp'rature" (II, ii), moves irre-
versibly towards the death Juliet gloomily predicts:

O God, I have an ill-divining soul!
Methinks I see thee, now thou art so low,
As one dead in the bottom of a tomb. (III, v)

And the fate which will claim its victims in *Bodas de sangre*
claimed Shakespeare's lovers, as the Friar makes clear:

A greater power than we can contradict
Hath thwarted our intents. (V, iii)

---

[8] García Lorca, *El público y Comedia sin título*, ed. R. Martínez
Nadal and M. Laffranque (Barcelona: Seix Barral, 1978), p. 114,
l. 926.

Lorca clearly shared with Shakespeare — and with Soph-
ocles — a tragic perception of events: the conviction that a
single circumstance, or a human weakness, can — as in the
case of *King Oedipus* — motivate a pattern of events which
can be resolved only in death. In *Bodas de sangre* from the
moment in the first scene when the Novio asks his mother
for the knife, from the moment when Leonardo is named as
the Novia's former suitor, we know that the two men are
connected and doomed by events which took place some twenty
years previously, when both were children. Lorca's debt to the
tragic mode also includes a formal element of Greek tragedy:
the Chorus, whose function he recognized and integrated into
the structure of his play, but whose identity he varied as he
naturalized it to fit without friction into his own dramatic frame-
work. In *Yerma*, which he told Juan Chabás would be "Una
tragedia con cuatro personajes principales y coros, como han
de ser las tragedias" (II, p. 1027), the Chorus's role of com-
menting on events and suggesting a solution is played by the
Lavanderas in Act II and by the Macho and Hembra in Act III.
In *Bodas de sangre* there are, as we shall see later, a series of
songs which operate as poetic commentaries on events. There
also appear in the third act the Leñadores, who, not involved
in the feud, can comment with apparent detachment on what
has happened, what is happening and what will happen. Woody
Allen's parody of a Greek tragedy, *God. A Play,* contains a
chorus who spurns his traditional function by stating timor-
ously: "We don't like to get involved." [9] Lorca's woodcutters
are most certainly involved; their objectivity is illusory, for it
is Lorca's ideas they voice and it is he who chose to put three
of them on stage: one for each year of the Madre's doomed
marriage and of the Novia's doomed courtship. What makes
their statements and songs important is that they do not speak
with a single voice; their varied and conflicting reactions to
events show Lorca's sensitive awareness that there can be no
single clear-cut response to people's actions or motives. Their
statements about fate, death and understanding give us much to

[9] Woody Allen, *Without Feathers* (London: Sphere Books, 1978),
p. 163.

think about. The third woodcutter's harping on discovery and
death — "Ya darán con ellos", "Pero los matarán", "Los bus-
can y los matarán" (III, i) — relates him most closely to Soph-
ocles' Chorus in *King Oedipus,* who warns that only when a
man is dead can he be called happy:

Then learn that mortal man must always look to his ending,
And none can be called happy until that day when he carries
His happiness down to the grave in peace.

   Gloomy as his predictions are, they are nevertheless tem-
pered by a very human doubt, as when he asks: "¿Crees que
ellos lograrán romper el cerco?" The second Leñador's reply
— "Es difícil. Hay cuchillos y escopetas a diez leguas a la
redonda" — sadly acknowledges that the lovers are unlikely to
find in others the understanding they arouse in him and which
he expresses in simple dicta and desperate hopes: "Hay que
seguir la inclinación; han hecho bien en huir"; "El cuerpo de
ella era para él y el cuerpo de él para ella"; "Hay muchas
nubes y será fácil que la luna no salga." But the first Leñador
— and Lorca — know that the moon will emerge from the
clouds to illuminate the lovers: and that knowledge, together
with the first Leñador's reminder that the Novio belongs to
a "casta de muertos en mitad de la calle," shows how unreal-
izable is the ideal of tolerance expressed in his dignified observation: "El mundo es grande. Todos pueden vivir en él."
   What makes these noble ideals of understanding and humanity so pathetic in *Bodas de sangre* is that the Leñadores who
voice them know them to be impossible; the appearance in the
same scene of the Mendiga — death — and the Luna — her
accomplice — dooms them to the failure predicted in their
songs about blood, moon and death. With the precise inevitability caused by their parallel structure, their songs to the
moon are modified into songs to death. The invocation of the
first Leñador:

                    ¡Ay triste luna!
                    ¡Deja para el amor la rama oscura!

is echoed by the second Leñador's appeal:

> ¡Ay triste muerte!
> Deja para el amor la rama verde.

The immediate shattering of the humane beliefs advocated by the woodcutters is part of a pattern of conflicts in *Bodas de sangre* between ideals and their defeat. Lorca makes no fewer than four of his characters — Madre, Criada, Padre and Mujer — define marriage in terms of enrichment and of security. The Madre's definition of marriage in the first scene as "Un hombre, unos hijos y una pared de dos varas de ancho para todo lo demás" is echoed by Leonardo's wife in her dream of "Aquí los dos; sin salir nunca y a levantar la casa" (II, i); it reverberates again in the song of the Criada:

> Porque llega tu boda
> recógete las faldas
> y bajo el ala del novio
> nunca salgas de tu casa. (II, ii)

Against this ideal of stability Lorca set the reality of widowhood, the fact of an unhappy marriage and the threat of the title: in the same way, the thrifty, careful living represented by the accumulation of money is challenged and defeated by the madness of uncontrollable passions, be they the powerful sexual impulses summarized as "inclinación" or the unquenchable thirst for blood and vengeance whose suddenness still marks the brutal vendettas of Sardinia and Sicily; under the headline "Sardinia murder in shepherd families' feud", *The Times* reported on 14th May, 1976:

> Two armed and masked men today stopped a lorry carrying 25 men to work in the mountains here, ordered one off and shot him dead. Police said it apparently was another murder in a 16-year-old feud between two shepherd families.

The "dos buenos capitales" mentioned by the Suegra (I, ii) which will be merged by the cool business deal transacted by the Madre and Padre are kept apart by fevered minds, by the "sinrazón" diagnosed by the Novia in the forest scene (III, i). By interweaving the passion of the Novia and Leonardo into the feud between two families, Lorca has given the past a key role in the shaping of people's lives. With her obsessive recollections, the Madre makes the bloody events of twenty years previously an integral and vibrantly menacing part of the play's texture, keeps them fresh and vivid before us with descriptions so graphic that the events could have happened the day before, as she recalls during the wedding ceremony:

> Cuando yo llegué a ver a mi hijo, estaba tumbado en mitad de la calle. Me mojé las manos de sangre y me las lamí con la lengua. (II, ii)

In the final scene the past tenses Lorca put repeatedly into her mouth relate to the immediate and not to the distant past as she recounts the deaths of her son and of Leonardo as an inescapable sentence pronounced before the play opened. Before the play began they were as doomed as Amargo, the hero of his 'Romance del emplazado'; their death was programmed for a special day, a "día señalado" not in the religious calendar but in the calendar of Fate:

> Vecinas, con un cuchillo,
> con un cuchillito,
> en un día señalado, entre las dos y las tres,
> se mataron los dos hombres del amor. (III, ii)

Lorca's repetition of "dos" in the last act acknowledges the indiscriminate power of death; the good are as vulnerable as the bad. Towards the end of *La zapatera prodigiosa* the lethal fight off-stage of two men over the blameless *zapatera* is reported with the same nonchalant conciseness:

VECINA ROJA

Dos hombres como dos soles.

VECINA AMARILLA

Con las navajas clavadas. (II, p. 314)

In *Bodas de sangre,* Leonardo's fatalistic warning:

> La misma llama pequeña
> mata dos espigas juntas (III, i)

is fulfilled in the Niña's song:

> Sobre la flor del oro
> traen a los muertos del arroyo.
> Morenito el uno,
> morenito el otro. (III, ii)

Both men, the wrongdoer and the wronged, are alike in death
as they never were, materially or emotionally, in life, and it is
death itself, in the person of the Mendiga, who equates them
systematically in deliberate indifference to right and wrong:

> Yo los vi; pronto llegan: dos torrentes
> quietos al fin entre piedras grandes,
> dos hombres en las patas del caballo.
> Muertos en la hermosura de la noche.
>
> Flores rotas los ojos, y sus dientes
> dos puñados de nieve endurecida.
> Los dos cayeron, y la novia vuelve
> teñida en sangre falda y cabellera.
> Cubiertos con dos mantas ellos vienen
> sobre los hombros de los mozos altos.
> Así fue; nada más. Era lo justo.
> Sobre la flor del oro, sucia arena. (III, ii)

The Mendiga represents and executes the grim justice of
death: if either man had survived the fight, he would have had
nothing to live for except the disgrace from which Casimiro
Pérez Pino fled, according to the *Heraldo de Madrid.* Shame
would have been the survivor's companion, as it is for some of
the mourners. The feud, revived by the passion of Leonardo
and the Novia, has claimed more victims in death and in life.

2. *People as prisoners*

ALTHOUGH the Niña's elegy to Leonardo and the Novio — "Morenito el uno, / morenito el otro" (III, ii) — makes them indistinguishable in death, Lorca differentiates them sharply and systematically in life. The persistent idealization of the Novio is matched by the relentless deprecation of Leonardo, who is praised when alive only by the Novio and when dead only by his wife. The Novio's generous remark to Leonardo's wife — "Tu marido es un buen trabajador" (II, ii) — comes after Leonardo's spiteful question, overheard by the Novia: "¿Y trajo ya el novio el azahar que se tiene que poner en el pecho?" (II, i). The Novio's innocent joy inspired by the *corona* — "¡Con la corona da alegría mirarte!" (II, i) — exposes the malice of Leonardo's remarks to the Criada: "¿La novia llevará una corona grande, no? No debería de ser tan grande. Un poco más pequeña le sentaría mejor" (II, i). The fact that the Novio chose a crown made of wax blossoms signals in his character a lack of spontaneity and an excess of caution which contrast with Leonardo's impulsive and passionate nature. Leonardo's rudeness to his mother-in-law in the second scene of the play contrasts with the Novio's deference to his mother, to whom he says dutifully: "¡Siempre la obedezco!" (II, i). The Novio is temperate, as his mother makes clear when refusing wine on his behalf: she says "No lo prueba" (I, iii). The Novio works diligently and productively amid his vines; Leonardo drifts from job to job. The Novio is a conformist who respects the rites and customs of society; Leonardo resents and rebels against them. The Novio is sexually innocent and is easily rebuffed by the Novia; Leonardo is sexually experienced and harbours a passion that nothing can still. The Novio is open, ingenuous, candid; Leonardo is moody, evasive with his wife and astutely disingenuous, as when he tells her with bogus incredulity:

> ¿Querrás creer? Llevo más de dos meses poniendo herraduras nuevas al caballo y siempre se le caen. Por lo visto se las arranca con las piedras. (I, ii)

The Novio's purchase of the vineyard (I, i) offers an example of thrift and industry which could never be followed by Leonardo, who allows himself the luxury of a horse even though his wife complains that "No tenemos dinero" ((II, ii) and even though he aggressively reproaches the Novia with his "dos bueyes y una mala choza" (II, i). His need of and dependence on his horse reveals a restlessness, a disquiet, at odds with the Novio's stolidity and equanimity, which is disturbed only when the past catches up with him and the spirits of his father and brother dominate him; it is only then that he sees his arm as useful for a task other than that of cutting vines:

> ¿Ves este brazo? Pues no es mi brazo. Es el brazo de mi hermano y el de mi padre y el de toda mi familia que está muerta. (III, i)

To have arms over which he exercises no control relates the Novio to the unfortunate Rafael, who, the Vecina informs the Madre, had both his arms cut off accidentally by "la máquina" (I, i). In offering to our minds the images of the hideously dismembered Rafael and the robot-like Novio whose arms are manipulated by his dead father and brother, Lorca is depicting — on different levels of suffering — the casualties of sudden violence; both men — one without arms and the other without life — justify the Madre's railing against "Todo lo que puede cortar el cuerpo de un hombre" (I, i).

No matter how different they are and people say they are, Leonardo and the Novio are linked; just as other characters in the play are connected by the ties of blood, the two men are fused by the spilling of it. Neither is free or independent; both belong to a family, both are members of a community, both are contained within that network of contacts and interrelationships

which in *Bodas de sangre* ensures that the Novia and Leonardo's
wife are cousins and that the Criada saw the marriage of the
Novio's grandfather (II, ii). The "mujeres que cogen las alcaparras" who told Leonardo's wife that they had seen him "al
límite de los llanos" (I, ii) are members of that ubiquitous,
voluble community which is as restrictive to his freedom of
action as his own heritage. The fact that Leonardo is one of the
four characters in the play whom Lorca represents as following
a pattern established by their forebears points to the sombre
conviction he shared with Quevedo in *La vida del Buscón* that
people are victims of their families. The Mujer's realization
that she is "despachada" leads her to remind us that "El mismo
sino tuvo mi madre" (II, i). The Novia, according to the Madre,
is a "Planta de mala madre" (II, ii), a woman who we were
told earlier "No quería a su marido" (I, i). The Novio's fate,
according to the first Leñador, was to belong to "su casta de
muertos en mitad de la calle" (III, i); whereas Leonardo is
forced to kill by his blood, which "Mana de su bisabuelo, que
empezó matando" (II, ii).

When they gossip and speculate harmlessly about the "medias caladas" in the first act (scenes i and ii), the Muchacha in
Leonardo's house and the Criada in the Novia's intrude upon
the lives of Leonardo and the Novia in a way that both resent.
Many people appear in *Bodas de sangre* and many more move
off-stage in the minds of characters. The reapers mentioned by
the Vecina (I, i), the "medidores del trigo" mentioned by Leonardo (I, ii) and the wedding guests who come from afar constitute a society that demands its ceremonies, imposes its rules
and exacts its price when they are infringed. The songs which
are sung in five of the seven scenes of the play represent the
ritualization of social customs as Lorca deliberately utilized
such traditional modes as the lullaby, the epithalamium and the
dirge. The institution of marriage and the punishment exacted
by a deeply conservative rural society for violating it are linked by Lorca's choice of the circle to show people encompassed
by the traditions and demands of society. The men who were
so festively eager to form a circle in order to "bailar la rueda"
after the wedding (II, ii) were those who manned "el cerco"
enclosing the Novia and Leonardo in the forest, which is both

a ring of men and a siege of attitudes. The guitars they so recently held have been replaced, according to the third Leñador's precise indication, by "cuchillas y escopetas a diez leguas a la redonda" (III, i).

What that menacing ring of armed men represents is the conformity demanded by a community, whose customs are shown by Lorca to be timeless and unchanging. The Madre's declaration — which will be echoed by Juan in *Yerma* and by Bernarda Alba — that "Las niñas no salen jamás a la calle" (II, ii) is as orderly and parrot-like as the perfunctory exchange of praises, claim and counter-claim with which she and the Padre agree to the marriage before the idea of *gustar* is even mentioned:

MADRE

Tú sabes a lo que vengo.

PADRE

Sí.

MADRE

¿Y qué?

PADRE

Me parece bien. Ellos lo han hablado.

MADRE

Mi hijo tiene y puede.

PADRE

Mi hija también.

MADRE

Mi hijo es hermoso. No ha conocido mujer. La honra más limpia que una sábana puesta al sol.

PADRE

Qué te digo de la mía. Hace las migas a las tres,
cuando el lucero. No habla nunca; suave como la
lana, borda toda clase de bordados y puede cortar
una maroma con los dientes.

MADRE

Dios bendiga su casa.

PADRE

Que Dios la bendiga. (I, iii)

The Novio is happy to live by such conventions; Leonardo
is not. Respect for customs and traditions does not save the
Novio from death, and Lorca's failure to praise or condemn
Leonardo reveals not equivocal moral values but his melancholy
conviction that the pressures of family and tradition are stronger
than the individual, and that goodness and decency are in themselves not enough to protect innocent victims from harm. At
the end of the play the Padre, dishonoured by his daughter, is
still suffering the consequences of marrying a woman who did
not love him. Leonardo's wife, obviously a good spouse and
mother, is unable to make Leonardo love her however hard
she tries to humour him and understand him, and we are left
with the bitter suspicion that Leonardo married her not because
of her intrinsic worth or attractiveness but because she was the
Novia's cousin, a fact she stresses when she tells the Novio:
"¡Que seas feliz con mi prima!" (II, ii). Although she attracts
our sympathy as the victim of Leonardo's marriage of spite,
Lorca's understanding of people under pressure makes her
act in a totally credible way. Her suspicions about her husband,
particularly apparent in her agitated questions during the wedding festivities (II, ii), are motivated by the love that makes
her defend him from her mother's hostility and exalt him when
he lies dead.

Lorca shows a similarly acute understanding of the Novia
when he directs her in one scene to bite her hand "con rabia"
and grip the Criada by the wrists (I, iii) and in another to throw

the orange blossom to the floor (II, i). With these impulsive acts of infantile pique, the Novia expresses her impotent dismay at her impending marriage to a man she does not love. Lorca shows not only the conflict within her, but, more painfully, her awareness of it, which makes her speech to the man who caused it full of tensions and contradictions:

> ¡Ay qué sinrazón! No quiero
> contigo cama ni cena,
> y no hay minuto del día
> que estar contigo no quiera,
> porque me arrastras y voy,
> y me dices que me vuelva
> y te sigo por el aire
> como una brizna de hierba. (III, i)

The fight between passion and scruples gives way in the last four lines above to a helplessness as both her mind and the flow of the sentence are hypnotized by Leonardo's will. Her appearance before him "en enaguas" and her retort "¿Qué más da?" to the Criada's reproach (II, i) show that for her modesty and decorum are irrelevant so far as her former suitor is concerned; her need to discharge her feelings is stronger than her sense of propriety. Although her father claims that "No habla nunca" (I, iii), her passion for Leonardo — be it expressed in recrimination, sensation or self-justification — gives her an eloquence, a vivid command of speech in contrast with the dry, curt words with which she addresses the Novio, particularly in the scene after their marriage. The Novio cannot arouse in her words warmer than "¡Quita!", "¡Ay! ¿Eras tú?", "¡Claro!" and "Déjame" (II, ii). If she tells him before they are married "Estoy deseando ser tu mujer y quedarme sola contigo, y no oír más voz que la tuya" (II, i), it is not because his voice is appealing and vibrant, but because it would replace the rich, magnetic voice of Leonardo. Only minutes earlier she had described in terms of sensuous idealism the deep effect Leonardo's voice has on her and her helplessness before the danger it threatens:

No puedo oírte. No puedo oír tu voz. Es como si me bebiera una botella de anís y me durmiera en una colcha de
rosas. Y me arrastra, y sé que me ahogo, pero voy detrás. (II, i)

Later, in the forest, her images of the chain around her
neck and of herself as a dog asleep at his feet (III, i) emphasize
the submissiveness, the lack of will which her own virtues are
unable to prevent. From being "buena ... Modosa. Trabaja-
dora" in the Madre's estimation (I, i), she becomes a "Víbora"
in her eyes (III, ii) because of a passion she was unable to
suppress. A victim — like Leonardo — of pride as well as of
passion, she can explain her feelings only in images and sensations; the effect Leonardo has on her is instantaneous and
erotic, as she makes clear in a brief statement which excludes
the mind and its reasoning:

> Que te miro
> y tu hermosura me quema. (III, i)

As José Alberich has acutely observed, the Novia "se siente
fuertemente atraída, más que por su prometido, tímido y virgen,
por su antiguo novio, es decir, por el hombre que despertó su
sensualidad adolescente y que además tiene ahora para ella el
aliciente de su experiencia sexual, por ser casado" (*1*, p. 21). At
the end of the play Lorca makes the Novia's forceful speech of
self-justification into an amalgam of disturbing sensations by
adding to the traditional fire of love images of a turbid river
and of birds, which, as Alberich makes clear (*1*, p. 27), tradition-
ally represent the penis in folklore:

> ¡Porque yo me fui con el otro, me fui! Tú también te
> hubieras ido. Yo era una mujer quemada, llena de llagas
> por dentro y por fuera, y tu hijo era un poquito de agua
> de la que yo esperaba hijos, tierra, salud; pero el otro era
> un río oscuro, lleno de ramas, que acercaba a mí el rumor
> de sus juncos y su cantar entre dientes. Y yo corría con
> tu hijo que era como un niñito de agua fría y el otro me
> mandaba cientos de pájaros que me impedían el andar y
> que dejaban escarcha sobre mis heridas de pobre mujer
> marchita, de muchacha acariciada por el fuego. (III, ii)

The Novia's awareness of her helplessness makes her into the prisoner of her feelings for Leonardo, which have achieved nothing more than to inflame an unsatisfied sexual desire and to make her into a virgin widow. In describing him as "un río oscuro" and "un golpe de mar", she suggests both his sexual drive and the menace it represents. His name acquires relevance and meaning for the Madre only when he is identified as one of "los Félix" (I, i); apart from the maimèd Rafael, Leonardo is the only character to whom Lorca gives a name rather than a generic label. Whereas labels such as Madre, Padre, Mujer and Suegra denote relationships that have meaning within a social context, Leonardo stands out because he is indifferent to those relationships. Not only is he qualified — and doomed — by his surname and his family, he is defined by his name, whose meaning was given in 1655 as "of a churlish disposition". [10] Had Lorca wanted to give him a label, Jinete, or Intranquilo, or Emplazado would have been more appropriate than Marido, for, as his first appearance on stage makes clear, he is not an ideal husband. His failure to eat at home, his early-morning rides, his lies to his wife and his rudeness to his mother-in-law reveal a truculent furtiveness which erupts into his exaggeratedly irascible response to the Muchacha's gossip about the stockings. His aggressive indifference to the Novia's gifts, far from convincing us or his wife of his lack of concern, show his raw nerves at the impending marriage of his former fiancée, his wife's cousin.

The same irascibility, this time exacerbated by hurt pride, makes his meeting with the Novia so acrimonious. To be the first to arrive is in itself tactless; to speak with such calculated pique releases the recriminations which pride had contained within him since they broke off relations. Presumably they have not spoken since then, although on his horse he has haunted her, as he did at the end of the first act when, unseen to the audience, he appeared at twilight outside the Novia's cave. In his sour allusions to "la plata" and "dos bueyes y una mala choza" (II, i), Leonardo implies that the Novia or her family

[10] E. G. Withycombe, *The Oxford Dictionary of English Christian Names*, 3rd ed. (1977), pp. 193-4.

did not regard him as a good match; and they were probably right, for the very impulsiveness which captivates and menaces her at the same time prevented him from settling into the routine of toil and thrift. Although the broken engagement still rankles in his mind, Leonardo's pride prevented him from trying either to better himself or to effect a reconciliation. Only too late has he discovered the hollowness of pride, which forced him into marrying a woman he did not love and in keeping silent about the woman he did love. His menacing prediction to the Novia — "El orgullo no te servirá de nada" — is followed by his avowal that, by accepting the tyranny of pride, he lost the chance to admire her:

> Callar y quemarse es el castigo más grande que nos podemos echar encima. ¿De qué me sirvió a mí el orgullo y el no mirarte y dejarte despierta noches y noches? ¡De nada! ¡Sirvió para echarme fuego encima! Porque tú crees que el tiempo cura y que las paredes tapan, y no es verdad, no es verdad. ¡Cuando las cosas llegan a los centros no hay quien las arranque! (II, i)

His agitated movements after the wedding confirm his belief that time cures nothing. As we follow his brusque, puppet-like movements, directions like "(Sale Leonardo)", "(Sale Leonardo y se sienta)", "(Mutis Leonardo por la derecha)" and "(Leonardo cruza al fondo)" translate into action his wife's perceptive analysis of him as someone restless and unsettled: "le gusta volar demasiado. Ir de una cosa a otra. No es hombre tranquilo" (II, ii). His escape on horseback with the Novia proves her right and justifies her tribute to him when dead as a beautiful horseman who

> Corrió ferias y montes
> y brazos de mujeres. (III, ii)

His self-justification in the forest is an attempt to illustrate through image and sensation his belief that "¡Cuando las cosas llegan a los centros no hay quien las arranque!" (II, i). Like the Novia, Leonardo is aware that what they feel and do cannot be rationalized and that they are drawn together by a force

against which the mind and common-sense are powerless to
act; cool, detached thinking is made impossible by a charge
of passion expressed in a powerfully erotic image:

> También yo quiero dejarte
> si pienso como se piensa.
> Pero voy donde tú vas.
> Tú también. Da un paso. Prueba.
> Clavos de luna nos funden
> mi cintura y tus caderas. (III, i)

His desire to forget her is thwarted — in a kind of special
pleading which shows that he is not thinking "como se pien-
sa" — by his horse, by the odour of her body and by the "sangre
negra" within him, which is a graphic symptom of that "distemp'rature" also afflicting Romeo:

> Porque yo quise olvidar
> y puse un muro de piedra
> entre tu casa y la mía.
> Es verdad. ¿No lo recuerdas?
> Y cuando te vi de lejos
> me eché en los ojos arena.
> Pero montaba a caballo
> y el caballo iba a tu puerta.
> Con alfileres de plata
> mi sangre se puso negra,
> y el sueño me fue llenando
> las carnes de mala hierba.
> Que yo no tengo la culpa,
> que la culpa es de la tierra
> y de ese olor que te sale
> de los pechos y las trenzas. (III, i)

The earth which impels Leonardo to a dangerous course of
action is the same earth which claims him and the Novio, for
it was his malaise that committed them both to what the Madre
calls a "lecho de tierra" (III, ii). The peace of mind the Madre
dreamed of in the first act when she stated that "yo quiero bor-
dar y hacer encaje y estar tranquila" (I, i) has been achieved
by the murder of her son and will henceforth be found in the

ritual transit between home and cemetery: "La tierra y yo.
Mi llanto y yo. Y estas cuatro paredes" (III, ii). Beyond the
play she will continue to be a prisoner of the grief to which she
has been totally committed for twenty years. As she crosses
herself at the end of the first scene, she senses — and prepares
herself for — the repetition of bloody events, and anticipates
with her simple but moving gesture the prayer intoned in the
final scene to the "dulce cruz" (III, ii). The knife she curses
at the beginning of the play is the knife she laments at the end,
and the idea implicit in the circular movement, that the dirge
is the consequence of the curse, points to a tragic flaw in her
nature. The very act of railing against the knife keeps it in focus
as the tool of hatred and vengeance; instead of banishing the
knife from her lips and making of it a taboo, she courts
disaster by naming it and vilifying it. In so doing, she ignores
the cautious fears of so many primitive peoples, studied and
documented by Sir James Frazer; in Madagascar, he reported:

> no soldier should eat an ox's knee, lest like an ox he
> should become weak in the knees and unable to march.
> Further, he should be careful to avoid partaking of a cock
> that died fighting or anything that has been speared to
> death. [11]

The Madre displays no such caution, either in mentioning
the hated instrument of death or in urging her son to pursue the
lovers; the conflict within her between fear for his life and
desire for revenge is quickly resolved in the anguished words:
"¡Anda! ¡Detrás! No. No vayas. Esa gente mata pronto y
bien... ; ¡pero sí, corre, y yo detrás!" (II, ii). Having lost her
husband and a son, the Madre accepts instinctively that she
may soon be lamenting the death of her remaining son. The
Madre is a disturbing character, and if her presence on stage
and the words she pronounces trouble the reader or spectator,
it is because Lorca understood and was able to depict the scars
left on her mind by grief. She is a totally credible character:
this is made clear by comparing Lorca's fictitious widow with

---

[11] *The Golden Bough*, Papermac Series, 54 (London: Macmillan,
1970; first publ. 1922), p. 28.

the widows and widowers who provided Colin Murray Parkes
with the case histories for his book *Bereavement*. So similar are
the Madre's symptoms to those documented by Parkes that her
character clearly evolved from Lorca's acute and sensitive observation of grief-stricken widows. In insisting that she has to
go to the cemetery "todas las mañanas" (I, i), she conforms to
Parkes's statement that "Most widows liked to visit their husband's grave and several spoke of the almost uncanny attraction
that drew them to the cemetery." Parkes's claim that "For the
bereaved person, time is out of joint" is corroborated by
the Madre, who oscillates constantly between the past and the
future, as when she tells her son: "Sí, sí, y a ver si me alegras
con seis nietos, o los que te dé la gana, ya que tu padre no
tuvo lugar de hacérmelos a mí" (I, i). The brevity of her married
life swells the dimensions of her husband's deeds and, as it
transforms hypothesis into confident fact, leads her to indulge
in the "idealization" and "retrospective distortion" documented
by Parkes. The Novio's retort that without water his father
could not have covered "los secanos" with trees is immediately
dismissed by his mother:

> Ya la hubiera buscado. Los tres años que estuvo ca-
> sado conmigo, plantó diez cerezos. (*Haciendo memoria.*)
> Los tres nogales del molino, toda una viña y una planta
> que se llama Júpiter, que da flores encarnadas, y se secó.
> (I, iii)

Parkes has pointed out perceptively of the bereaved person
that "Besides assuming a new identity, it is necessary to give
up the old." [12] This is precisely what the Madre does not do
as she clings to the past and to vivid memories of her dead son
and dead husband. Her remark to the Novia — "Que tengo la
cabeza llena de cosas y de hombres y de luchas" (II, ii) — reveals a mind committed to conflict and tired in its dedication to
grief. In nurturing herself on grief and hatred, the Madre has
done as much as anyone in the play to ensure that more blood
will be spilt. Her protectiveness towards her son when the

---

[12] Colin Murray Parkes, *Bereavement: Studies of Grief in Adult
Life* (Harmondsworth: Penguin, 1976), pp. 70, 95, 91, 160, 116.

3. *Colour*

As the curtain falls on the final scene of mourning, the tearful women, "arrodilladas en el suelo", observe through their reverential pose Lorca's direction that the simple room in which the last scene is played "tendrá un sentido monumental de iglesia". They kneel overawed in a room similar in size to a church and suggestive in its clinical whiteness of a mortuary or mausoleum. Lorca's insistence on the brilliant whiteness and on the architectural solidity of the setting creates a flatness of perspective which throws into relief the women who have been brought together by the spilling of blood, which is represented at the beginning of the final scene by the red yarn:

> Habitación blanca con arcos y gruesos muros. A la derecha y a la izquierda escaleras blancas. Gran arco al fondo y pared del mismo color. El suelo será también de un blanco reluciente. Esta habitación simple tendrá un sentido monumental de iglesia. No habrá ni un gris, ni una sombra, ni siquiera lo preciso para la perspectiva. (III, ii)

In *La casa de Bernarda Alba* the play of black against white in a static situation is Lorca's way of representing visually the lack of warmth, hope or variation in the lives of women ruled by an intransigent mother. His deliberate exclusion of colour from the setting of the final scene of *Bodas de sangre* shows the importance he assigned to colours throughout his tragedy, where the contrast of black and white fundamental to *La casa de Bernarda Alba* is enriched by a range of colours, lighting effects and chromatic impressions, from the shining face of the Novia's mother (I, i) to the ashen face of the Novio (III, ii). The colouring and decorations devised for the three rooms into which the first act is divided are the most evident indication of the role Lorca gave to colours in his dramatic design and purpose.

Throughout *Bodas de sangre* he coloured and varied his scenes so distinctively that the spectator's passage from place to place is corroborated visually by the different hues or props or backgrounds he sees. Joined by grief and death, the three widows will return from the clinically white room in which Lorca placed them at the end of the play to the three houses which he situated side by side and so clearly differentiated in the first act. The Madre will return to her "Habitación pintada de amarillo" (I, i); Leonardo's widow will go back to her more home-like and warmly toned "Habitación pintada de rosa con cobres y ramos de flores" (I, ii); and the Novia will no doubt confine herself in her *cueva,* where flowers and curtains and fans and mirrors and jugs break up fussily the cold whiteness of the walls:

> Interior de la cueva donde vive la Novia. Al fondo, una cruz de grandes flores rosa. Las puertas redondas con cortinas de encaje y lazos rosa. Por las paredes de material blanco y duro, abanicos redondos, jarros azules y pequeños espejos. (I, iii)

Lorca's reasons for distinguishing chromatically between the three homes is simple: by showing them to be different in appearance and in colour, he also suggests the emotional and physical gulf separating those who inhabit them. The diverse colours we see in such large expanses in the first three scenes — yellow, pink and white — will separate the three homes in the minds of the spectator.

Lorca's use of colours in *Bodas de sangre* is so carefully organized as to demonstrate that his artist's sense of composition is matched by a painter's sense of tone and contrast. His use of colours is at the same time highly subtle; the spectator can easily connect the pink bows and flowers in the Novia's cave with the pink walls of Leonardo's house, but he will have to divine for himself Lorca's motives for repeating — and reducing — that colour in the home of the woman who poses a threat to whatever marital harmony there may be between Leonardo and his wife. After placing the three houses and the major characters side by side in the first act, Lorca in the second act moves the characters, and particularly the Novia, outwards from her *cueva,* seen in fading light at the end of the first act, firstly into the nocturnal gloom of the "Zaguán de la casa de la Novia" (II, i) and thence into the open air. The exterior setting in which he places his characters is no idyllic landscape of lush green and purling river, but a hard, forbidding mountain setting coloured sombrely in grey, blue and dull brown:

> Exterior de la cueva de la Novia. Entonación en blancos grises y azules fríos. Grandes chumberas. Tonos sombríos y plateados. Panoramas de mesetas color barquillo, todo endurecido como paisaje de cerámica popular. (II, ii)

The blue which is found both inside and outside the Novia's home — in the jugs and in the landscape — is a hue to which Lorca resorts in both scenes of the final act. In the first scene, set simply in a "Bosque", Lorca's specification — "Es de noche" — repeats the words and the gloom with which he opened the second act: "Zaguán de la casa de la Novia. Portón al fondo. Es de noche" (II, i). At the end of the first act, Lorca carefully directed that "La luz va desapareciendo de la escena" in order to herald Leonardo's appearance — unseen to the audience — on horseback. The common denominator of these scenes of darkness is therefore Leonardo, whose nocturnal rides anticipate, and somehow invite, his death at night.

The darkness which enfolds the two lovers in the forest is relieved only by the moon, whose three appearances on stage are marked by a strong blue light, which Lorca describes in turn as "un vivo resplandor azul", "la luz azul intensa" and "una fuerte luz azul". Having thus established a chromatic link between where the Novia lives and where she flees to with Leonardo, Lorca links both settings with the white room in the final scene, in which he places two Muchachas "vestidas de azul oscuro" (III, ii). By the use of colour rather than words, Lorca has succeeded in associating the Novia with the Fates — and with death.

The colours he places before our eyes are many and varied;
but they acquire greater depth and significance when we tone
them with the colours we are asked to visualize in metaphor,
image and song. In *Bodas de sangre* Lorca has devised a constant interplay, in operation from the first to the last scene,
between colours he puts before our eyes and colours he conjures
up in our imaginations. The colours he chooses do not corre-
spond to a simple code; the care with which he uses them
enables us to make connexions between place and place, person
and person, place and person. But his colours also tell a story,
point a moral; their deliberate ambivalence allows us to ponder
on life and death and on the speed with which the first yields
to the second.

As many of the colours found in *Bodas de sangre* belong to
the flowers, plants and trees he names, Lorca exploits both the
hues and the associations they have acquired in popular and
cultured poetry. By making the first Leñador bewail the "Muerte
de las hojas grandes" and the "Muerte de las secas hojas" (III, i),
he reminds us that all trees — and men — can die; his lament,
together with the Madre's elegy to her son as "flores secas"
(III, ii), echoes the words and the intention of Garcilaso, who
warned in his sonnet 'En tanto que de rosa y d'azucena' that
"Marchitará la rosa el tiempo helado". [13] Lorca is not as explicit
as Garcilaso; colours, and the flora and fauna to which they
belong, are in themselves an eloquent comment on the narrow
line between life and death. This is particularly true of the
first colour Lorca puts before us: yellow.

In the early scenes of the play Lorca encourages us to as-
sociate yellow with marriage and fertility; the Madre tells her
son that she will give his fiancée the yellow-coloured "pendientes
de azófar" (I, i); and the "gran cadena de oro" worn by the
Novio when he visits the Novia (I, iii) is matched by the "lazos
de oro" with which, according to a lyric commentary, he fastens
the Novia's crown:

> La novia
> se ha puesto su blanca corona,

[13] Garcilaso de la Vega, *Poesías castellanas completas,* ed. Elias L.
Rivers (Madrid: Castalia, 1969), p. 59.

> y el novio
> se la prende con lazos de oro. (II, i)

The gold objects he wears or handles thus identify him in the
eyes of others as a creature of gold and justify the hyperbolic
tribute to him repeated in the preliminaries to the wedding:

> El novio
> parece la flor del oro. (II, i)

However, the speed with which gold can be tarnished is
signalled in the final scene in a statement that is as explicit
and informative as a stage direction; the Mendiga's triumphant
declaration "Sobre la flor del oro, sucia arena" is immediately
chorused and elaborated by the two Muchachas and the Niña:

MUCHACHA 1.ª Sucia arena.
MUCHACHA 2.ª Sobre la flor del oro.
NIÑA.   Sobre la flor del oro
              traen a los muertos del arroyo.
              Morenito el uno,
              morenito el otro.
              ¡Qué ruiseñor de sombra vuela y gime
              sobre la flor del oro! (III, ii)

The vision of gold buried in sand evokes the victory of death
and decay over life and beauty with a graphic immediacy
duplicated in the Madre's lament for her dead son: alive he
was the "Girasol de tu madre"; dead, he lies "con los labios
amarillos" (III, ii). The Madre had already associated yellow
with death when she related to the Padre her reactions to the
death of her elder son:

> Cuando yo llegué a ver a mi hijo, estaba tumbado en
> mitad de la calle. Me mojé las manos de sangre y me
> las lamí con la lengua. Porque era mía. Tú no sabes lo
> que es eso. En una custodia de cristal y topacios pondría
> yo la tierra empapada por ella. (II, ii)

This linking of earth and the yellow-coloured topaz is
paralleled in the final scene by the association of wheat and

death, which, put into the mouths of the Mendiga and the
Madre, underlines once more the intimate relationship between
them; soon after the Mendiga asks the Muchachas for "Un
pedazo de pan", the Madre glorifies wheat for being enriched
by the bodies of her sons:

> Benditos sean los trigos, porque mis hijos están debajo
> de ellos; bendita sea la lluvia, porque moja la cara de
> los muertos. (III, ii)

Wheat is as much subject to the laws of nature as man. The
Madre's dictum "Los hombres, hombres; el trigo, trigo" (I, i)
points to the common fate preached by Leonardo in his metaphoric connexion of wheat and fire:

> La misma llama pequeña
> mata dos espigas juntas. (III, i)

In the same way as the gold chain worn by the Novio and
the gold bows he put into the Novia's hair bring to mind the
expanse of yellow against which the first scene was enacted,
so the cross of large pink flowers and the pink bows tying the
curtains in the Novia's cave repeat on a small scale the pink
walls of Leonardo's house. The delicacy suggested by the
colour pink is of course directly related to the rose. In Leonardo's house Lorca had already used the rose to suggest natural beauty and fragility when the Mujer and the Suegra lulled
the baby to sleep with the refrain "Duérmete, rosal..."; in the
same scene he made the Muchacha gossip excitedly about the
"medias caladas" the Madre and her son had bought for the Novia; after pointing to her thigh with the words "y aquí una
rosa", she exclaims in wonder: "¡Una rosa con las semillas y
el tallo!" (I, ii). The tender beauty represented by the rose
will be very much in the Novia's mind when she reacts to
Leonardo's voice, which induces in her — according to Lorca's
acute interpretation of her feelings — a swooning intoxication
and a slumber on the perfumed softness of roses:

> No puedo oír tu voz. Es como si me bebiera una botella
> de anís y me durmiera en una colcha de rosas. (II, i)

The Novia will enjoy few such moments of sensual self-indulgence. These sensations are blissful; roses are beautiful; children are beautiful; all are subject to the whims and ravages of death, as Calderón insisted in his sonnet 'Estas que fueron pompa y alegría':

> A florecer las rosas madrugaron,
> y para envejecerse florecieron... [14]

Lorca makes the same point, but in a more oblique way, when he matches the "cruz de grandes flores rosa" we actually see in the Novia's cave with images of two crosses, one of ashes and the other of the poisonous oleanders, which once more equate Leonardo and the Novio in the eyes of death. The Suegra's instruction to her daughter:

> Sobre la cama
> pon una cruz de ceniza
> donde estuvo su almohada,

is as chillingly evocative of a life cut short as the wish expressed by the Madre a few minutes later as she addresses her dead son:

> Que te pongan al pecho
> cruz de amargas adelfas. (III, ii)

In the final scene, even though he scrupulously banishes colour from the backcloth, Lorca parades a number of strong hues against the stark white walls: the dark blue of the dresses of the Muchachas and the red yarn they are unwinding; the dark green garb of the Mendiga, "totalmente cubierta", we were told in the previous scene, "por tenues paños verdeoscuros"; and the black shawl worn by the Novia. The blue dresses take our minds back to the blue jugs in the Novia's cave, to the blue-tinted landscape outside it and to the blue light cast by the Moon. The chromatic consistency between the Luna and the Muchachas shows Lorca's independence of mind and

[14] *The Oxford Book of Spanish Verse*, 2nd ed. (1940), p. 236.

his ability to control and adapt his sources; according to Robert
Graves, in Greek myths "the Moerae, or Three Fates, are the
Triple Moon-goddess — hence their white robes, and the linen
thread which is sacred to her as Isis". [15] Having chosen to give
his moon a blue hue, he ensured that his own Fates had robes
that match it. He also ensured that the imagery of his play
reinforce this association of blue and death, which he had
already made in *Así que pasen cinco años* (1931) and which
he was to repeat in *Doña Rosita la soltera* (1935). In the first
play the colour merely hints at death in the first Jugador's
melancholy commentary that "La vida se le escapa por sus
pupilas, que mojan la comisura de sus labios y le tiñen de
azul la pechera del frac" (II, p. 452). In the second play the
colour explicitly denotes death as Rosita solemnly recites the
language of flowers:

> Las amarillas son odio,
> el furor, las encarnadas;
> las blancas son casamiento,
> y las azules, mortaja. (II, p. 801)

When the Novia sees the violent death of Leonardo as the
only cure for her fevered mind and body, it is the blue of his
veins and a violet-edged shroud that colour her desperate
thoughts:

> Estas manos, que son tuyas,
> pero que al verte quisieran
> quebrar las ramas azules
> y el murmullo de tus venas.
>
> Que si matarte pudiera,
> te pondría una mortaja
> con los filos de violetas. (III, i)

The broken veins imagined by the Novia will soon be a
fact confirmed by two striking images of the blood-stained
Novia and Novio which give lethal point to the red yarn of the
Muchachas. We have been so conditioned by constant visions

---

[15] *The Greek Myths* (Harmondsworth: Penguin, 1978), I, p. 48.

of blood spilt and prophesies of blood to be spilt that it may come as a suprise to realize that the red yarn is the first time that Lorca actually puts the colour before our eyes instead of before our imagination. The first Muchacha's allusion to the "Novio carmesí" and the Mendiga's announcement to her that

> la novia vuelve
> teñida en sangre falda y cabellera (III, ii)

justify the play's prophetic title: the blood shed after the wedding was not the blood of the Novia's virginity of which the Criada sang expectantly:

> Porque el novio es un palomo
> con todo el pecho de brasa
> y espera el campo el rumor
> de la sangre derramada. (II, ii)

There is no escape from mentions and pictures of blood in this play; and the shedding of it is reported or predicted in a succession of gory echoes which combine image with cold statement. In chanting as part of their lullaby that

> La sangre corría
> más fuerte que el agua, (I, ii)

the Suegra and the Mujer summarize the bloody prehistory of the play with a simple fact which the Madre elaborates when, in describing to the Padre the sight of her dead elder son, she likens blood to a fountain:

> Por eso es tan terrible ver la sangre de uno derramada
> por el suelo. Una fuente que corre un minuto y a nos-
> otros nos ha costado años. (II, ii)

The second Leñador also knows what the Madre saw with her own eyes: "Pero sangre que ve la luz se la bebe la tierra" (III, i). In pleading with death "¡No abras el chorro de la sangre!" the same woodcutter echoes both the Madre's vision of a fountain of blood and the Luna's desperate longing for

"esta fuente de chorro estremecido". The Luna's thirst for
blood — expressed in his gory fantasy of cheeks red with blood
— has its precedent in reality in the Madre's licking of her
son's blood. The Madre's mind is dominated by red: the red
of the blood she has seen spilt and of the blood she knows
will be spilt. She also remembers her dead son and husband as
"dos geranios" and recalls — with a tribute which will also be
applied to Leonardo's infant son — that "tu padre... me olía
a clavel" (I, i). Even the trees and flowers her husband planted,
from the "diez cerezos" to "una planta que se llama Júpiter",
give red flowers (I, iii). Lorca associates the Novio with the
manly vigour — and with the bloody fate — of his father and
brother when he inserts "clavelinas" into the lyric eulogy intoned by the third Muchacha before the wedding:

> El novio
> parece la flor del oro;
> cuando camina,
> a sus plantas se agrupan las clavelinas. (II, i)

In the Criada's dreams of marital bliss the Novio is imagined
as "un palomo / con todo el pecho de brasa" (II, ii). This vision
of the Novio inflamed by desire is complemented in the final
act by the "fuego" felt by the Novia in Leonardo's presence
(III, i) and by her description of herself as "una mujer quemada" (III, ii). Just as man's strength, represented by the carna-
tion and geranium, is drained by the shedding of blood, so will
the fire of passion subside and cool into the ashes so often
found in Golden Age poems about the brevity of life. The
incandescent glow of passion is replaced in our minds by the
cold greyness of dead ashes in "La cara color ceniza" of the
Novio and in the "cruz de ceniza" to be placed over Leonardo's
bed (III, ii). The "valles grises" which occur in the lullaby are
identified in the "valles de ceniza" of the Luna (III, i) and are
associated visually with the "blancos grises" we see for our-
selves in the landscape framing the Novia's cave (II, ii).

The "Grandes chumberas" Lorca placed in the same landscape prepare us visually for the forest to which the lovers
flee and — chromatically — for the appearance of the Mendiga.

To dress the Mendiga in green is visually effective as she blends into the trees; it also shocks us into the realization that, if green is the colour of lush nature, it is also the colour of death, which claims as its victims men, plants, flowers and trees. By her presence and by her words the Mendiga confirms and complements the fate predicted by the second Leñador in his simple assurance: "Un árbol de cuarenta ramas. Lo cortaremos pronto" (III, i). This doomed tree mocks the optimistic songs sung by the wedding guests, who visualize love and marriage in terms of a colourful and productive nature:

> Que despierte
> con el ramo verde
> del laurel florido.
> ¡Que despierte
> por el tronco y la rama
> de los laureles! (II, i)

The promise of the flowering laurel is destroyed by the "amargo laurel" found in the second Muchacha's song (III, i). The love of Leonardo and the Novia is no more free to express itself in the forest than in the community to which they belong; the second woodcutter's appeal:

> ¡Ay triste muerte!
> Deja para el amor la rama verde (III, i)

is rejected by the Luna when Lorca makes him admonish the branches:

> No quiero sombras. Mis rayos
> han de entrar en todas partes,
> y haya en los troncos oscuros
> un rumor de claridades,
> para que esta noche tengan
> mis mejillas dulce sangre. (III, i)

In the final scene the lethal associations aroused by the dark blue dresses, the red wool and the dark green robe are rounded off when the Novia joins the mourning women "sin azahar y

con un manto negro" (III, ii). In her sombre garb she joins the
cortège of black-clad figures who have crossed the stage, from
the Madre and the Novio in the first act to a nameless woman
in the third. She also reminds us most vividly of herself attired
for her wedding in a black dress and — according to the second
Muchacha's song — "botas de charol y plata" (II, i). Her rapid
transition from bride to widow is thus commemorated visually
on stage by a black shawl which replaces her white crown, and
by the black gown formerly worn for a wedding in Galicia at
least; as one Galician has recalled, "aquí era la boda de negro
siempre. Los zapatos de boda eran los zapatos que llevaban
para la sepultura." [16]

The Novia, whom we must assume to be still wearing her
black wedding gown, is dressed after the death of Leonardo and
her husband not for the grave but for widowhood and the living
death of social disgrace. The unrelieved black of her robe,
shawl and shoes stands out against the brilliant whiteness of
her surroundings in visual confirmation of the disaster which
had been hinted at in the lullaby with its images of black water
and black blood. The Suegra's disturbing chant:

> El agua era negra
> dentro de las ramas

echoes in the graphic symptom Leonardo confessed to the Novia:

> Con los alfileres de plata
> mi sangre se puso negra. (III, i)

In mentioning the silver pins over which the Muchachas
squabbled excitedly, Leonardo reveals the fascination still ex-
ercised on his mind by the Novia's crown of orange blossoms,
which had forced him to ask the rancorous question: "¿La
novia llevará una corona grande, no?" (II, i). From the moment
earlier in the same scene when the Novia throws the orange
blossom to the floor, Lorca keeps the crown in focus: we see

---

[16] Carmelo Lisón Tolosana, *Antropología cultural de Galicia* (Madrid: Siglo Veintiuno de Editores, 1971), p. 325.

it on the floor, on the Novia's head both in her home and in the forest. We hear it mentioned by Leonardo, the Novio and the Madre, and celebrated throughout the second act in a series of songs begun by the Criada:

> Despierte la novia
> la mañana de la boda.
> ¡Que los ríos del mundo
> lleven tu corona! (II, i)

The Novia's throwing of the blossom to the floor was merely a rehearsal for her definitive rejection of married respectability which leads the Madre to upbraid her as a "Floja, delicada mujer de mal dormir" who "tira una corona de azahar para buscar un pedazo de cama calentado por otra mujer" (III, ii). The Novia has thus emptied of all meaning the lyrical tributes to her in the second act as "la blanca novia", a "blanca doncella" and a "blanca niña"; because of the flight of the Novia, a newly married woman, with Leonardo, a married man, the whiteness so consistently evoked in the second act in the mentions of "corona", "azahar", "camisa de nieve", "jazmines en la frente" and "paloma" will be succeeded in the third act by a series of images that evoke not virginal whiteness but the coldness of emotional and physical death. The white sheet to which the Madre proudly likened her son's honour (I, iii) — and which the Novia mentioned to Leonardo as proof of her virginity (III, i) — is transformed into a winding-sheet as the Madre, addressing her dead son, longs for a

> sábana que te cubra
> de reluciente seda... (III, ii)

The Madre's admonition to the Novia "Ligera como paloma debes ser" (II, i) urges on her a soaring expectancy which she herself echoes and thwarts in her promise: "Yo haré con mi sueño una fría paloma de marfil que lleve camelias de escarcha sobre el camposanto" (III, ii).

With her mentions of an ivory dove and camelias of frost, the Madre presents herself as one more victim of the cold which had chilled the Luna and the horse of the lullaby; the "crines heladas" (I, ii) attributed to the horse is elaborated by the Luna into an anguished lament:

> ¡Vengo helada
> por paredes y cristales! (III, i)

And the Mujer's lament:

> ¡Ay dolor de nieve,
> caballo del alba! (I, ii)

is vivified in the Luna's vision of being transported on the back of snow as hard as jade, whose green colour puts us in mind of the Mendiga:

> Pero me lleva la nieve
> sobre su espalda de jaspe... (III, i)

Lorca makes a direct connexion between snow and death in two verbal pictures which are at the same time miniature allegories; when he makes the Mendiga gleefully describe the teeth of the two corpses as "dos puñados de nieve endurecida" and follows the Mujer's tribute to her dead husband "Era hermoso jinete" with the epitaph "y ahora montón de nieve" (III, ii), Lorca records not simply the death of two men but the certainty of total extinction like snow melting into earth.

In his *Remarks on Colour* Ludwig Wittgenstein states his belief that colours cannot be explained:

> When we're asked "What do 'red', 'blue', 'black', 'white', mean?" we can, of course, immediately point to things which have these colours — but that's all we can do: our ability to explain their meaning goes no further. [17]

Even if we accept Wittgenstein's reservations and go only so far as he allows, we can still point to so many things possessing

[17] *Remarks on Colour*, trans. Linda L. McAlister and Margarete Schättle (Oxford: Blackwell, 1977), p. 29e.

colours in *Bodas de sangre* that their incidence and their recurrence clearly respond to a specific purpose in Lorca's dramatic design. His rich chromatic range is such a skilful and sophisticated feature of his craftsmanship that it stands out as a major beneficiary of the five years' thought he gave to his tragedy. What is remarkable about his use of colours is his instinctive awareness that a colour cannot have a single meaning, and he recognized and exploited the ambivalence of colours and our diverse responses to them by evoking in our minds visions of red flowers and blood, of verdant nature and Death attired in green. In *Bodas de sangre* colours aid and illustrate Lorca's profoundly pessimistic beliefs; they are essential to its visual appeal and to its tragic meaning.

4. Space, movement and structure

THE rich diversity of nature conveyed by Lorca's mentions of flowers, weeds, trees, vines and olives is underscored by the geography outlined by Lorca, which, far from pinpointing the places where the action occurs, opens up in our minds vistas of space embracing coast and mountains, forest and plains. By merely naming these different areas and features, Lorca separates people physically and temperamentally; the "gente de la costa" who amused the Novio because they were frightened of horses (II, ii) invite contrast with Leonardo, whose dependence on his horse is total. And while the Novia inhabits the hard, inclement lands named as "los secanos", her mother came, she tells us, "de un sitio donde había muchos árboles. De tierra rica" (II, i).

The geography of *Bodas de sangre* is both vague and symbolic, and its symbolic meaning is reinforced by Lorca's eye for a simple but telling detail. The women who saw Leonardo far from his home, "al límite de los llanos" (I, ii), were picking "alcaparras," capers, which grow, as Lorca knew, in the most barren lands of Valencia, Murcia and Andalusia. The capers are thus a minute feature of the harsh terrain whose proximity to the Novia and whose remoteness from the other characters are constantly stressed. After being asked by his wife whether it was he who had been seen "al límite de los llanos", Leonardo retorted with a lie and with a rhetorical question to which he could have found no answer: "No. ¿Qué iba a hacer yo allí, en aquel secano?" (I, ii). His lie — exposed by the state of his horse, which was "reventando de sudor" — takes our minds towards the Novia and her cave, where in the following scene the Novio responds to his mother's complaint about "Cuatro horas de camino y ni una casa ni un árbol" with the placid, resigned words: "Estos son los secanos" (I, iii). When the Niña stands in the doorway in the final scene of the play and intones her symbolic commentary:

> El hilo tropieza
> con el pedernal, (III, ii)

she associates the thread of life about to be cut with the Novia's habitat, summarizing with "el pedernal" the Padre's description of the unyielding land on which they live and with which they fight:

> Esta tierra necesita brazos que no sean pagados. Hay que sostener una batalla con las malas hierbas, con los cardos, con los pedruscos que salen no se sabe dónde. (II, ii)

The Novia and Leonardo flee from this land of rocks and weeds to the contrasting opulence of the forest. The choice of areas as distinct as woodland and rocky terrain shows quite simply that the lovers can find no release in nature — or in this life; in the forest they are doomed by the presence of the river, which flows through the play as a geographic fact and as the symbolic threat underlying the Criada's song:

> Giraba,
> giraba la rueda
> y el agua pasaba. (II, ii)

Lorca had already indicated that the Novia's cave can be reached by following a river and that a stream marks one way of going from her home to the church; this association of the Novia and flowing water gives point both to the Madre's complaint — "Yo estoy ya vieja para andar por las terreras del río" (I, iii) — and to the Criada's precise estimate of the distance between the cave and the church as "Cinco leguas por el arroyo, que por el camino hay el doble" (II, i). The river reappears as the route taken by the Novio to the forest in pursuit of the lovers; while some of the pursuers approach "por la cañada", according to the Luna, the Novio follows the course of the very river that will drown his and Leonardo's screams when they knife each other. The Mendiga's confident prediction that

> El rumor del río
> apagará con el rumor de troncos
> el desgarrado vuelo de los gritos, (III, i)

establishes between the river, the trees, the Mendiga and the Luna a complicity which Lorca strengthens in the final scene in the song of the first Muchacha and in her conversation with the Mendiga. In her lament:

> Amante sin habla.
> Novio carmesí.
> Por la orilla muda
> tendidos los vi,

the first Muchacha illustrates the idea of death as the leveller of all men by imagining lover and bridegroom prostrate — as on a mortuary slab — on the bank of the stream that had marked the Mendiga's passage from the forest to the house presented in the final scene. To the first Muchacha's question "¿Vienes por el camino del arroyo?" the Mendiga replied emphatically: "¡Por allí vine!" (III, ii).

If rivers and streams are the means by which people approach and find others, they also represent the way in which all people are taken out of this life. With the two rivers and two streams which cross the landscape of *Bodas de sangre*, Lorca gives dramatic life to the symbol defined with such simple dignity by Jorge Manrique in his *Coplas por la muerte de su padre*:

> Nuestras vidas son los ríos
> que van a dar en la mar,
> qu'es el morir. [18]

Rivers and streams, as they connect the lives and destinies of the major characters, are a feature of the play's infrastructure,

---

[18] Jorge Manrique, *Cancionero*, ed. Augusto Cortina, 4th ed. (Madrid: Clásicos Castellanos, 1960), p. 90 (stanza 3).

which — unlike the linear pattern of *La casa de Bernarda Alba* — explores space and depends on the distances travelled by characters and so often mentioned by them. A cumulative impression of disconnected lives is created by the Padre's mentions of separated lands and far-off church (I, iii), by the songs heard in the distance (II, i), by the presence at the wedding of "gente de la costa" (II, ii), and by the threat — mentioned by the second Leñador — of "cuchillos y escopetas a diez leguas a la redonda" (III, i). This distance — about fifty-five kilometres, or thirty-four miles — had been mentioned in the first scene of the play, where the Vecina told the Madre that the Novia lived "a diez leguas de la casa más cerca". Between the Vecina's further remark that the Novia "Vive sola con su padre allí, tan lejos" (I, i) and the Mendiga's reply to the Novio that she comes "De allí..., de muy lejos" (III, i), the word *lejos* points repeatedly to the distances dividing people in life — and to the ultimate separation of death.

The countryside in which Lorca situates *Bodas de sangre* is vast and unchanging; timeless and nameless, it offers him an extensive backcloth against which to project characters disturbed by emotional rather than by social or political tensions. Lorca disdained the attempt made by Jacinto Benavente in *Señora ama* (1908) to give his play a bogus authenticity by reproducing country speech. He also avoided the moral and sententious posture struck by Antonio and Manuel Machado, who made Don Diego comment disdainfully in *La Lola se va a los puertos:*

> ¡El absentismo es la plaga
> de Andalucía y la muerte
> de nuestra riqueza agraria!
> ¿Hay nada más cursi que esos
> labradores... que no labran?... [19]

No one could glean from *Bodas de sangre* even the faintest hint of the ten strikes of farm workers which took place between February and May 1932 in the provinces of Cádiz, Córdoba, Huelva and Sevilla. The violent events Lorca dramatized in

[19] Manuel and Antonio Machado, *Obras completas*, p. 473.

his first tragedy occur in a timeless cocoon remote from and
apparently oblivious of the bloody incident of Casas Viejas
(Cádiz), in January 1933, when a Captain Rojas ordered the
machine-gunning of a defiant group of peasants who had de-
posed the mayor and killed two civil guards. [20]

In perpetuating some of the traditions governing marriage
and death, Lorca presents a countryside frozen in time. The
Madre and the Padre arranged the marriage of their son and
daughter according to the time-honoured ritual which Michael
Kenny observed in Castile:

> Once the decision to marry has been taken the *novio*
> (prospective bridegroom) and his parents come to the
> house of the *novia* (prospective bride) to ask her parents
> formally for her hand. The traditional gift to the girl at
> this stage is a bracelet, but this varies if there is a prized
> family heirloom to be passed on and may take the form
> of a ring or even a diadem. There is no formal ceremony;
> the visit usually takes place at about 7 p.m., the hour
> of the *merienda,* of which the visitors partake. From this
> moment onward, the boy and girl are mutually committed
> to marriage, which takes place very soon afterwards. [21]

The Andalusian custom by which "La boda se ha de efectuar
en las primeras horas de la mañana o al entrar la noche" is
respected when we see the Novia preparing for her wedding
"de noche" (II, i). [22] And the Mendiga's report that Leonardo

---

[20] Manuel Tuñón de Lara, *La II República* (Madrid: Siglo Veintiuno de Editores, 1976), vol. I, pp. 107, 132. For a fuller treatment of
agricultural unrest in Andalusia in the 1920s and 1930s, see Tuñón de
Lara, *Luchas obreras y campesinas en la Andalucía del siglo XX. Jaén
(1917-1920). Sevilla (1930-1932)* (Madrid: Siglo Veintiuno de Editores,
1978). The Andalusian countryside is still troubled; so much is clear
from a recent article by Antonio Ramos Espejo — 'El campo andaluz
puede estallar' (*Triunfo,* no. 866, 1st September 1979, pp. 16-19) — and
from the recent declaration of the Socialist Senator Plácido Fernández
Viagas: "El paro es el terrorismo de Andalucía" (reported in *El Día*
[Santa Cruz de Tenerife], 6th September, 1979).

[21] *A Spanish Tapestry: Town and Country in Castile* (London:
Cohen and West, 1961), p. 67.

[22] Machado y Álvarez, *Biblioteca de las tradiciones populares españolas,* I, p. 80.

and the Novio "vienen / sobre los hombros de los mozos altos" (III, ii) relates them to the unnamed woman whose death and funeral are narrated by Bécquer in his *rima LXXIII*:

> De la casa en hombros
> lleváronla al templo,
> y en una capilla
> dejaron el féretro.
> Allí rodearon
> sus pálidos restos
> de amarillas velas
> y de paños negros.

Those who bore the three corpses observed part of a ritual that can be taken as far as the cemetery, as the following account establishes:

> El cadáver, encerrado en el ataúd, a que el pueblo llama, habiendo consideración a su forma, *guitarra* o *violín*, es conducido a hombros desde la casa mortuoria hasta la salida de la ciudad, y allí es depositado en *el carro de los muertos*, si el cementerio está distante. [23]

Lorca needed the open country and the agelessness represented by its customs and traditions in order to illustrate the conflict between personal, emotional liberty and the stability contained within a house; he also needed it in order to allow Leonardo and the Novia scope and space in which to flee before placing the Novia in a room whose similarity to a mortuary or a mausoleum reminds us that death awaits those who try to elude their tragic destiny. Leonardo's defiance of society, expressed in his aggressive claim

> que no me importa la gente,
> ni el veneno que nos echa, (III, i)

[23] Bécquer, *Obras completas*, 11th ed. (Madrid: Aguilar, 1964), p. 482; Machado y Álvarez, *Biblioteca de las tradiciones populares españolas*, I, pp. 94-5.

draws him, the Novia and the Novio away from the three
houses placed side by side in the first act. Separated by Leonardo in the sequence of scenes in the first act, the Novio and
the Novia will be parted permanently by Leonardo at the end
of the second act. Having moved the action outwards from the
Novia's cave into the open air — and towards death —, Lorca
returns the bereaved survivors to an indoor setting in a circular
sweep which matches in structure the "rueda" of the dancers
and the "cerco" of the pursuers. The structure of *Bodas de
sangre* plots a search for emotional and physical freedom that
fails.

Leonardo is the most restless character in the play, and in
order to rove as far and as incessantly as he does he relies
totally on his horse, which, as Juan Villegas has aptly stated,
"cabalga a lo largo de todo el drama" (*20*, p. 22). As I shall
show more fully in the next chapter, there is more than one
horse: there is the horse of symbol, which moves in the minds
of the characters and readers and is important for what it represents; and there is a real horse — and its rider — which
people hear and see. It is this real horse that connects five
consecutive scenes as it transports Leonardo in each one of
them: from his house (I, ii) to the Novia's cave (I, iii; II, i),
from the Novia's cave to the forest (II, ii; III, i). The fact that
Leonardo is the "jinete" recognized by the Novia at the end
of the first act and eulogized by the Mujer at the end of the
third is a key factor in the structure and in the action of the play.
The Criada's question to the Novia — "¿Sentiste anoche un
caballo?" — is answered at the end of the first act by the repetition of that sound off-stage: ("Se siente el ruido de un caballo)" (I, iii). Leonardo's horse gives him his mobility, and
his dependence on it and his ruthless use of it are conveyed by
the repeated idea of the gallop. Leonardo rides as frenetically
as Rivas's Romantic hero, Don Álvaro, who — according to a
witness — galloped at night "como alma que llevan los demo-
nios" (I, iv). The Suegra's question — "pero ¿quién da esas
carreras al caballo?" (I, ii) — reverberates in the Criada's blunt
comment to Leonardo: "Vas a matar al animal con tanta carrera" (II, i). And her recrimination echoes in turn in the Novio's
conjecture, when neither Leonardo nor his horse can be found,

that "Debe estar dándole una carrera" (II, ii). The precarious freedom Leonardo achieves by means of his horse is recognized by the couple he divides; the Novio's avowal in the forest that "No hay más que un caballo en el mundo" (III, i) focuses belatedly on the very horse that enabled Leonardo to haunt and menace his fiancée, as she acknowledged in her knowing dictum that "Un hombre con su caballo sabe mucho y puede mucho" (II, i). When she escapes with him on his horse, "abrazados, como una exhalación" according to his wife (II, ii), she takes advantage of the animal he had used to threaten her honour with his long, frenzied rides — the same horse that will lead him to his death. That death is clearly prophesied on another level in the *nana* which encloses the second scene of the play, in which the minds and fears of the Mujer and the Suegra revolve consciously and unconsciously around Leonardo's horse.

Although Leonardo is the character who moves furthest, fastest and most compulsively in the play, Lorca surrounded the major characters with many people who fulfil different functions: social in the case of the unspecified number of wedding guests, symbolic in the case of the Muchachas and the Niña. The striking visual appeal of *Bodas de sangre* is due in large measure to Lorca's skill at placing and manipulating characters, whether in groups or reduced to an individual alone on stage. In the first scene the appearance of the Vecina, who brings the news of Rafael's hideous mutilation and identifies the Novia as Leonardo's former fiancée, casts a shadow over the action which will extend as far as the parallel intrusion of the Mendiga into the final scene; the disaster unwittingly hinted at by the former will be gleefully confirmed by the latter.

There is a great deal of movement in *Bodas de sangre*; there are also some memorable tableaux as Lorca displays his flair for composition; the combination of movement and stylized scenes contributes to the restlessness, the disquiet, of the tragedy. When at the end of the first scene Lorca directs that the Madre "En medio del camino se detiene y lentamente se santigua", he slows down her action, in itself solemn, so deliberately as to engrave it on our minds, which are thus conditioned to relate her action to the Mendiga's dominance of the stage at the end of the forest scene: she stands with her back

to the audience, opens her cloak and remains in the centre of
the stage "como un gran pájaro de alas inmensas". In their
stylized formality some scenes are reminiscent of paintings; the
arrangement of the marriage by the Madre and the Padre is as
stiffly formal as a number of paintings by José Gutiérrez So-
lana, such as *La visita del obispo, La familia* and *El retorno
del indiano*. With their skein of yarn the Muchachas bring to
mind Velázquez's painting *Las hilanderas*; and the final spec-
tacle of the weeping "vecinas, arrodilladas en el suelo" is reminiscent of a favourite theme of religious painting, the 'Pietà'.

Although it is these visually powerful scenes that impress
themselves on the mind, others are testimony of Lorca's skill at
creating a taut, nervous atmosphere by the number of exits and
entrances he disposes for his characters. Aided by the peculiar
light radiated by the Luna, the scene in the forest is tense and
menacing as Lorca interweaves symbolic and real characters
in a kind of cortège as they appear or reappear in the following
order: Leñadores; Luna; Mendiga; Luna; Novio and Mozo;
Novio (with Mendiga); Leñadores; Leonardo and Novia;
Luna. Lorca had devised a similarly choreographic pattern of
movement in the second scene of the second act, where he
imagined "un animado cruce de figuras". The abrupt exits and
entrances of the Novia, the Criada, the Novio, Leonardo and the
Mujer create a tension which is intensified by the guests, excitedly unaware with their "algazara y guitarras" of the emotional
strain felt by the major characters. It is these excited guests
who at the end of the scene break the circle of the dance, pour
onto the stage and then — responding to the call of their
blood — segregate themselves into two groups. In directing that
"La gente se separa en dos grupos", Lorca dramatizes simply
but forcefully the confrontation of two hostile factions which
the Madre identifies in the words she addresses to the Padre
at the end of the act:

> Vamos a ayudar a mi hijo. Porque tiene gente; que son
> sus primos del mar y todos los que llegan de tierra aden-
> tro. ¡Fuera de aquí! Por todos los caminos. Ha llegado
> otra vez la hora de la sangre. Dos bandos. Tú con el tuyo
> y yo con el mío. ¡Atrás! ¡Atrás! (II, ii)

These two bands perpetuate and only slightly modify the feud between the Madre's family and the Félix family: the Madre's family is the constant in them both and Leonardo is the link between them. Even if the Novia had fled with another man, Leonardo — married to a cousin of the Novia — would have been drawn into the feud on the Novia's side. He cannot avoid facing the Novio and his cousins across a divide of hatred. This new feud, which — like the one to which it is connected — will claim the lives of two men, is one more link in an apparently endless chain of violence from which there is no escape. As the Novia tells Leonardo as she passes sentence on him, "No hay nada que te defienda..." (III, i).

5. *Speech, poem and song*

I HAVE already suggested that Lorca fostered the illusion of space in order to remove his characters from three separate houses and to restore the survivors to them after death ended the bid for social and emotional freedom. Yet the geographic expanse against which his characters move is challenged and constricted by the play's infrastructure of verbal echoes harking back to the immediate or distant past. The "medias caladas" suggested as a gift by the Madre in the first scene are reported by the Muchacha as already bought in the second scene, where the brusque response which the mention of them elicits in Leonardo helps to define his nature. And the stockings are mentioned yet again, by the Criada in the Novio's house (I, iii). The triple mention of these stockings not only shows the passage of time and the transit of news, but connects the lives of characters who are physically divided. Leonardo says "Quita" and "Déjame" to his wife (I, ii); later, the Novia says "Quita" and "Déjame" firstly to the Criada (I, iii) and then to her fiancé (II, ii). The use of the same curt words is as precise a symptom of their common agitation as the silence they demand from others in boorish, curt displays of ill-tempered disquiet. Leonardo's brusque command to his wife — "¿Te puedes callar?" (I, ii) — reverberates both in the Novia's cry of "¡Cállate!" to her servant (I, iii) and in the command of "¡Calla!" he issues to the Novia in the forest (III, i).

By making his characters repeat seemingly innocuous facts and words, Lorca charges them with significance. The "carreras" of Leonardo — mentioned by the Suegra (I, ii), the Criada (II, i) and the Novio (II, ii) — recur as a consistent symptom of his malaise and as an omen of his frantic flight with the Novia. The triple allusion to the Novia and Mujer as cousins, however

innocent it may sound on the lips of the Vecina (I, i) and the
Mujer (I, ii; II, ii), points to a closely-knit community unified
by the ties of blood and menaced by the spilling of it. The
reader cannot escape the patterns of insistent echoes, which
are heard not simply when people communicate in dialogue but
when they express themselves in poems and in songs. To recognize these multiple echoes is both disquieting and depressing,
for the reader finds himself enclosed within an intricate network
of words, phrases and motifs which restricts his vision, obliging
him to connect, for example, the "pedrada en la frente" suf-
fered metaphorically by the Madre in the first scene with the
"golpe en las sienes" felt by the Novia after her wedding (II, ii).
Similarly, we ought not to be surprised when the Madre calls
the Novia a "¡Víbora!" (III, ii); she had already used the
serpent to create a sense of foreboding when she told her son
in the first scene "No sé . . . cómo yo dejo a la serpiente dentro
del arcón".

In the poem 'El grito', from *Poema del cante jondo*, Lorca
imagined a shout as an elegant arc curving across the night sky:

> La elipse de un grito
> va de monte
> a monte.
>
> Desde los olivos,
> será un arco iris negro
> sobre la noche azul. (I, p. 159)

In the prophecy of the Mendiga those graceful curves are to
and jagged; in her prediction that

> El rumor del río
> apagará con el rumor de troncos
> el desgarrado vuelo de los gritos, (III, i)

she states blandly but inaccurately that the river will
the sounds we shall actually hear at the end of the scene
moment when the two men meet off-stage and kill each
"dos largos gritos desgarrados". With these shrill, a
shrieks still resounding in our ears, we pass in the las

of the play to the poetic commemoration of the "grito" as a
deep root probed by a knife so small as to fit into the palm
of a hand:

> Vecinas, con un cuchillo,
> con un cuchillito,
> en un día señalado, entre las dos y las tres,
> se mataron los dos hombres del amor . . . .
> Y apenas cabe en la mano,
> pero que penetra frío
> por las carnes asombradas
> y allí se para, en el sitio
> donde tiembla enmarañada
> la oscura raíz del grito. (III, ii)

The roar of pain is thus in *Bodas de sangre* both a motif
and an actual sound, a shrill testimony to the sudden violence and brutal suffering which can befall any one at any
time. Before the screams of agony of the two men, we had
already heard on- and off-stage a series of sounds whose variety
contributes to the phonic richness of the play: Leonardo's horse
galloping away from the Novia's *cueva* at the end of the first
act; the "aldabonazos" made by Leonardo on his arrival at
the *cueva* (II, i); the "Voces cantando muy lejos" as Leonardo
half-heartedly answers the Criada's questions (II, i); the guitars
and then the "guitarras, palillos y panderetas" played before
the wedding (II, i); the "dos violines" in the forest, with which
Lorca devises a stylized, dirge-like counterpoint to the guitars
of the wedding scene as he exploits the association of stringed
instrument, shout and wind he had made in his poem 'El grito':

> Como un arco de viola
> el grito ha hecho vibrar
> largas cuerdas del viento. (I, p. 159)

These sounds are an essential part of the phonic variety
of the play, which is enriched by the many different ways in
which people speak and sing. Unlike the lacklustre and pre-
dictable verse penned by Zorrilla and the Machado brothers,
the verbal texture of *Bodas de sangre* is so varied that, as char-

acters speak in cold prose or in electrically charged poems, the reader or spectator is never allowed to become accustomed to a particular style or manner. Lorca's fine ear for dialogue, allied with his understanding of people's emotions and sufferings, make the many conversations of the play so diverse in their contrasts. Through dialogue Lorca distinguishes sharply between couples united by convenience or economic advantage and a couple drawn together by turbulent passions. If we listen to the exchanges between Leonardo and his wife in the first and second acts, we sense in the probing questions and recriminations of the Mujer and in the curt, evasive answers of Leonardo a partnership devoid of warmth and harmony; and it is in the house of her cousin, the woman who has undermined her marriage, that the Mujer recognizes its failure in a short but bitter confrontation with Leonardo:

MUJER

Vamos.

LEONARDO

¿Adónde?

MUJER

A la iglesia. Pero no vas en el caballo. Vienes conmigo.

LEONARDO

¿En el carro?

MUJER

¿Hay otra cosa?

LEONARDO

Yo no soy hombre para ir en carro.

MUJER

Y yo no soy mujer para ir sin su marido en un casamiento. ¡Que no puedo más!

LEONARDO

¡Ni yo tampoco!

MUJER

¿Por qué me miras así? Tienes una espina en cada ojo

LEONARDO

¡Vamos!

MUJER

No sé lo que pasa. Pero pienso y no quiero pensar. Una cosa sé. Yo ya estoy despachada. Pero tengo un hijo y otro que viene. Vamos andando. El mismo sino tuvo mi madre. Pero de aquí no me muevo. (II, i)

The similarly clipped, staccato phrases which make up the conversation between the Novia and Novio after their wedding reveal them as a similarly ill-matched couple menaced by the malaise afflicting both Leonardo and the Novia; as tense as Leonardo, the Novia reacts brusquely and nervously to her husband's embrace:

NOVIA

¡Quita!

NOVIO

¿Te asustas de mí?

NOVIA

¡Ay! ¿Eras tú?

NOVIO

¿Quién iba a ser? (*Pausa.*) Tu padre o yo.

NOVIA

¡Es verdad!

NOVIO

Ahora que tu padre te hubiera abrazado más blando.

NOVIA

¡Claro!

NOVIO *(la abraza fuertemente de modo un poco brusco)*

Porque es viejo.

NOVIA

¡Déjame! (II, ii)

The fragile relationships of Leonardo and his wife and the Novio and his new bride are accentuated stylistically by setting their brittle, curt exchanges against the vibrant, emotionally charged conversations of Leonardo and the Novia, in which the incidence of image, metaphor and simile reveals emotions fighting to emerge from years of proud silence. Leonardo's tactlessly early arrival at the *cueva* and his distempered allusions to the Novia's crown provokes between them a fiery exchange of recriminations in which they can express their feelings only by resorting to images of fire and of a bed of roses:

LEONARDO

Callar y quemarse es el castigo más grande que nos podemos echar encima. ¿De qué me sirvió a mí el orgullo y el no mirarte y dejarte despierta noches y noches? ¡De nada! ¡Sirvió para echarme fuego encima! Porque tú crees que el tiempo cura y que las paredes tapan, y no es verdad, no es verdad. ¡Cuando las cosas llegan a los centros no hay quien las arranque!

NOVIA *(temblando)*

No puedo oírte. No puedo oír tu voz. Es como si me bebiera una botella de anís y me durmiera en una colcha de rosas. Y me arrastra, y sé que me ahogo, pero voy detrás. (II, i)

The next time we see them together is in the forest; having
fled after the Novia's marriage to another man, they have for-
feited social respectability and have invited the death and disgrace spoken of before their appearance on stage by the Leñadores, Mendiga, Luna and the Novio. As the last people to
appear on stage in the forest scene, they recognize themselves
as outcasts and fugitives from a community they have outraged.
Leonardo's first word — "¡Calla!" — begins a conversation that,
violent in tone, content and feeling, is sustained by thoughts
and images of aggression. The Novia's rejoinder to Leonardo's
order to be silent is to lament the fire she feels in her head and
the glass splinters she senses on her tongue, and to plead for a
shotgun with which to end a relationship she represents as
a chain:

> Con los dientes,
> con las manos, como puedas,
> quita de mi cuello honrado
> el metal de esta cadena,
> dejándome arrinconada
> allá en mi casa de tierra.
> Y si no quieres matarme
> como a víbora pequeña,
> pon en mis manos de novia
> el cañón de la escopeta.
> ¡Ay, qué lamento, qué fuego
> me sube por la cabeza!
> ¡Qué vidrios se me clavan en la lengua! (III, i)

As it recalls the fire mentioned by Leonardo, the fire lamented by the Novia establishes between their first and second en-
counters a bond of emotional intensity as both lovers strive to
express their troubled awareness of conflicting emotions in
images which, unlike the vehement dialogue of their first en-
counter, are now channelled into the traditional mould of the
romance. Throughout their poetic dialogue in the forest, the as-
sonance on *é-a* underpins rhythmically the declarations of violent and passionate feelings that can only be evoked in images.
In their impassioned dialogue the flow and surge of poetry
carries them along; as they talk in images and set them within

a rhythmic pattern, they give the impression of having relinquished control over their reason, which is less powerful than
poetry. By making them talk in poetry, Lorca lifts Leonardo
and the Novia off the level of commonplace humanity and raises
them to the status of tragic lovers in the mould of Romeo and
Juliet. With the stage directions "(La abraza fuertemente)",
"(La arrastra)", "(abrazándola)" and "(Salen abrazados),." Lorca
punctuates their dialogue with a series of impulsive actions
which represent the irresistible physical attraction they feel for
each other combated the whole time by their confused awareness that their passion is mad. It is this blend of magnetism
and revulsion that makes their speeches so disturbed and disturbing. Even though she feels the fire of passion, which echoes
as a painful refrain, the Novia dreams colourfully of destroying
Leonardo by snapping his veins and clothing him in a shroud:

> Estas manos, que son tuyas,
> pero que al verte quisieran
> quebrar las ramas azules
> y el murmullo de tus venas.
> ¡Te quiero! ¡Te quiero! ¡Aparta!
> Que si matarte pudiera,
> te pondría una mortaja
> con los filos de violetas.
> ¡Ay, qué lamento, qué fuego
> me sube por la cabeza! (III, i)

Leonardo is prey to equally contradictory sensations and
impulses; when Lorca made him lament "¡Qué vidrios se me
clavan en la lengua!", he put into his mouth the symptom he
had attributed to the Novia in order to prepare us for statements that are similarly aggressive. Black blood and weeds and
the painful sensation of throwing sand in his eyes come to his
mind when he represents as a kind of disease of the body and
mind his failure to drive the Novia out of his thoughts:

> Y cuando te vi de lejos
> me eché en los ojos arena.
> Pero montaba a caballo
> y el caballo iba a tu puerta.

> Con alfileres de plata
> mi sangre se puso negra,
> y el sueño me fue llenando
> las carnes de mala hierba. (III, i)

His mind is so firmly cast in a mould of violent thought that
he even evokes the dawn chorus and daybreak in terms of sharp
edges and destruction; the verb "quebrarse" comes to his mind
as instinctively as it did to the Novia's:

> Pájaros de la mañana
> por los árboles se quiebran.
> La noche se está muriendo
> en el filo de la piedra. (III, i)

As they perpetuate Spain's rich ballad tradition, these dense-
ly textured poems — together with the Luna's soliloquy —
demand of the actors a solemn mode of declamation; they
occupy a point midway between speech and the songs intoned
in the play. The songs sung in five of its seven scenes are
woven inextricably into its fabric as Lorca commemorates
simple activities that are both timeless and universal; the fact
that characters sing when they do — when lulling a child to
sleep, or celebrating a marriage, or unwinding a skein of wool —
is totally credible and dramatically effective. The songs sung in
Bodas de sangre mark the passage from birth to death as they
range from the *nana* sung to Leonardo's child in the first act,
through the wedding songs in the second to the dirges intoned
in the third.

Although the individual songs of *Bodas de sangre* fulfil a
precise function at the moment of being sung, they are inter-
related by motifs and symbols whose recurrence helps to make
them into a poetic gloss on the events. The Leñadores' laments
about "la muerte mala" claiming "la verde rama" reach back
to the lullaby sung in the first act (scene i), and to the Criada's
song in the second (scene ii). The Leñadores' association of
love with leaves and dark branches in the first series of songs
is as sinister as the water dammed and blackened by branches
in the lullaby sung by the Suegra:

El agua era negra
dentro de las ramas.
Cuando llega al puente
se detiene y canta. (I, ii)

In the song sung by the Criada at the beginning of the second act, the wedding which has just taken place leads her to hope for the same branches to be separated, for water to be released and flow unchecked and for moonlight to glow with life and movement:

Giraba,
giraba la rueda
y el agua pasaba;
porque llega la boda
que se aparten las ramas
y la luna se adorne
por su blanca baranda.
Giraba,
giraba la rueda
y el agua pasaba.
¡Porque llega la boda,
deja que relumbre el agua! (II, ii)

The cold white moon is another motif linking songs in the three acts. The second Leñador's vision of "Plata en la cara de la novia" gives a sinister twist to this popular song:

¡Quién fuera rayo de luna,
para entrar por tu ventana,
irme arrimando, arrimando,
y platearte la cara! [24]

The metallic threat implicit in silver recalls the image of the moonbeam in the horse's eyes as "un puñal de plata", which Lorca associated in the *nana* with injury and flowing blood:

Las patas heridas,
las crines heladas,

[24] Enrique Llovet, *Magia y milagro de la poesía popular*, Libros de Actualidad Intelectual, 28 (Madrid: Editora Nacional, 1956), p. 221.

dentro de los ojos
un puñal de plata.
Bajaban al río.
¡Ay, cómo bajaban!
La sangre corría
más fuerte que el agua. (I, ii)

This *nana* offers a clash between content and intention; it draws attention to the presence of an innocent child and to Leonardo's parental responsibilities at the same time as it shows in images those responsibilities menaced by the sinister elements and omens of the images. As Lorca recalled in his lecture 'Las nanas infantiles' (I, p. 1081), he heard and noted in Granada six versions of this lullaby:

A la nana, nana, nana,
a la nanita de aquel
que llevó el caballo al agua
y lo dejó sin beber.

Lorca's elaboration of that song and his use of it to frame a scene in which Leonardo's horse is talked about establishes a close connexion between the creatures of fact and fantasy. Leonardo's horse is essential to his moods and his movements, and the development and dénouement of the play depend on the freedom it gave him to haunt the Novia and then escape with her. Leonardo's horse, "reventado de sudar", according to his wife, and "con los ojos desorbitados", according to the Suegra (I, ii), is as exhausted and abused as the horse of the *nana,* with its "patas heridas", its "crines heladas" and its "belfo caliente". Any rhythmic solace provided by this *nana* is chilled by its content, which lacks the warmth of this traditional English lullaby with its soothing tempo, comforting repetitions and "pretty li'l horses":

Go to sleep baby child,
Go to sleep my li'l baby.
Hush-a-by don't you cry,
Go to sleep my li'l baby.
When you wake you will have

All the pretty li'l horses,
Black an' blue, sorrel too,
All the pretty li'l horses.
Black an' blue an' sorrel too,
All the pretty li'l horses.
Hush-a-by don't you cry.
Go to sleep, my li'l baby. [25]

What Leonardo's child hears, without understanding what he hears, is a song about a horse that, clearly disturbed, weeps and refuses to drink of black water:

Nana, niño, nana
del caballo grande
que no quiso agua.
El agua era negra
dentro de las ramas.

Duérmete, rosal,
que el caballo se pone a llorar. (I, ii)

If the child is blissfully ignorant of the malaise and menace contained in the lullaby, the women who sing it are not, and the sinister images of their song are as ominous as the precise reminiscences of death we hear in the previous scene on the lips of the Madre. The vision of the weeping horse looks ahead to a horse that will be without a master — and to a child that will be without a father. With its frozen sweat and heated snout, the horse of the song shades into the horse of reality in the forest scene, where the Luna, using similar images of heat and cold, promises to light up the beast on which the lovers are escaping:

Yo haré lucir al caballo
una fiebre de diamante. (III, i)

The songs intoned by the guests before the wedding follow the model of such traditional songs of tribute as:

[25] William Engvick (ed.), *Lullabies and Night Songs* (London: Bodley Head, 1965), pp. 42-3.

> ¡Ay que el novio y la novia es bella!
> él es lindo y linda es ella.

and:

> Esta novia sí que es novia,
> ésta, que las otras no;
> ésta se lleva la gala,
> ésta se lleva la flor. [26]

The songs Lorca puts into the mouths of so many people do not constitute a single joyful chorus; they punctuate the second act, separating the acrid quarrel of Leonardo and the Novia, the Madre's declaration of hatred and the Mujer's troubled suspicions. In this way they create a counterpoint of tension, an atmosphere of brittle gaiety whose falseness is shown by Leonardo's dutiful voicing of a couplet that mentions the crown about which he had earlier been so caustic:

> La mañana de casada
> la corona te ponemos. (II, i)

Lorca's imagination has transcended and enriched the simple, candid tributes of popular song, which provides the idea but not the content of such beautiful lines as:

> Despertad, señora, despertad,
> porque viene el aire lloviendo azahar.

and:

> Despierte la novia,
> que por los campos viene
> rodando la boda,
> con bandejas de dalias
> y panes de gloria.

[26] Julio Cejador y Frauca, *La verdadera poesía castellana*, I (Madrid: Tip. de la Revista de Archivos, Bibliotecas y Museos, 1921-6), no. 299; Eduardo M. Torner, *Lírica hispánica: relaciones entre lo popular y lo culto* (Madrid: Castalia, 1966), p. 194.

The intrinsic beauty of such songs, as well as the hope they
express of awakening to a new phase of love and natural beauty,
are threatened by the bride herself and by the presence of
Leonardo as a guest. The life and hope they celebrate are trun-
cated in the third act firstly in the songs of the Leñadores and
then in the songs of the two Muchachas and the Niña. After
the Leñadores' conversation about Leonardo, the Novia and
the Novio, the incipient moonlight inspires in them a series
of poetic laments and moving pleas for the lovers to be left
concealed in the security of dark branches:

LEÑADOR 1.°

¡Ay luna que sales!
Luna de las hojas grandes.

LEÑADOR 2.°

¡Llena de jazmines la sangre!

LEÑADOR 1.°

¡Ay luna sola!
¡Luna de las verdes hojas!

LEÑADOR 2.°

Plata en la cara de la novia.

LEÑADOR 3.°

¡Ay luna mala!
Deja para el amor la oscura rama.

LEÑADOR 1.°

¡Ay triste luna!
¡Deja para el amor la rama oscura! (III, i)

When they reappear, the complicity of the Luna and Mendiga
has been established and the Mendiga's claim on the Novio has
been made clear in her longings to see him "dormido" and

"tendido" (III, i). The Moon is thus so unequivocally identified with death in the minds of the Leñadores that their laments consolidate the theme of death by a simple change of word from "luna" to "muerte":

LEÑADOR 1.º

> ¡Ay muerte que sales!
> Muerte de las hojas grandes.

LEÑADOR 2.º

> ¡No abras el chorro de la sangre!

LEÑADOR 1.º

> ¡Ay muerte sola!
> Muerte de las hojas secas.

LEÑADOR 3.º

> ¡No cubras de flores la boda!

LEÑADOR 2.º

> ¡Ay triste muerte!
> Deja para el amor la rama verde.

LEÑADOR 1.º

> ¡Ay muerte mala!
> ¡Deja para el amor la verde rama!

By duplicating the exact structure of his lines and changing only a few significant words, Lorca closes all escape routes in the reader's mind, enclosing us in a *cerco* of words and rhythms in the same way as he places Leonardo and the Novia in an actual *cerco* of men and weapons.

In keeping with her age, the Niña is active and curious, and her movement to and from the door of the church-like dwelling in which the last scene is enacted enables her to connect the Muchachas' songs with what is happening outside; their unwinding of the red wool is an allegorical re-enactment of the deaths which took place at the end of the previous scene. After the deaths the Mendiga leaves the dangerous forest and calls as a beggar at the house in order to relate "con delectación" the double murder to the Muchachas and Niña, whose songs to the thread of life are thus corroborated and complemented by the Mendiga's presence and her words:

> Yo los vi; pronto llegan: dos torrentes
> quietos al fin entre piedras grandes,
> dos hombres en las patas del caballo.
> Muertos en la hermosura de la noche. (III, ii)

Their songs are linked by three parallel questions, simple gambits in the game of life and death whose gravity clashes with their sing-song introductory formula common to childhood rhymes and riddles like "Caracol, caracol..." and essential to verbal games like:

> —Bexato, bexato
> ¿que levas n'o papo?
> —Leite callado... [27]

These are the questions put to the skein of wool:

> Madeja, madeja,
> ¿qué quieres hacer?

> Madeja, madeja,
> ¿qué quieres cantar?

> Madeja, madeja,
> ¿qué quieres decir? (III, ii)

The answers given by the *madeja* to the first question resemble a series of riddles whose common denominator is death and dreams of the impossible:

[27] Francisco Rodríguez Marín, *Cantos populares españoles* (Sevilla: Álvarez, 1882-3), I, no. 119; Machado y Álvarez, *Biblioteca de las tradiciones populares españolas*, IX, p. 185.

> Jazmín de vestido,
> cristal de papel,
> nacer a las cuatro,
> morir a las diez.
> Ser hilo de lana,
> cadena a tus pies
> y nudo que apriete
> amargo laurel.

In this reply Lorca compresses motifs found in popular songs and in the wedding songs sung in the second act. The "laureles" which, like the lush "ramo verde", are emblematic of the Criada's hopes, have become bitter and are choked by the chain and knot of marriage mentioned in *cantos populares* such as these:

> La cadena del amor
> tiene recios eslabones
> y el que llega a entrar en ella
> tarde sale de prisiones.
>   Y yo, como enamorado,
> en esa cadena entré;
> cuando quise salir de ella,
> prisionerito me hallé.
>
>   Entré en la iglesia moza,
> salí casada;
> no hay quien desate el nudo
> de esta lazada.
> Nudo tan fuerte,
> que nadie lo desata
> sino la muerte. [28]

Lorca's reduction of life to six hours and two brief lines — "Nacer a las cuatro, / morir a las diez" — is a melancholy echo and abridgement of yet another popular song that plots the progress of life through twelve hours:

> A la una nací yo,
> a las dos me bautizaron,

[28] Rodríguez Marín, *Cantos populares españoles*, II, no. 2013; III, no. 5752.

> a las tres ya tuve novio,
> a las cuatro me casaron,
> a las cinco tuve un hijo,
> a las seis le bautizaron,
> a las siete va a la escuela,
> a las ocho le enseñaron,
> a las nueve cayó quinto,
> a las diez cayó soldado,
> a las once se murió,
> a las doce le enterraron. [29]

The same melancholy telescoping of life occurs in the reply to the second question, where the songs urging the Novia to awake are echoed and answered by the certainty of "velar"; the sepulchral meaning of watching over a corpse is implicit in Lorca's mention of grief and wounds of wax, recalling the Novia's waxen orange blossoms:

> Heridas de cera,
> dolor de arrayán.
> Dormir la mañana,
> de noche velar.

And the Niña, in answer to the same question, follows the thread out into the freedom of nature, represented by "el pedernal" and "los montes azules", towards the inevitability of death, symbolized by the knife and the removal of the bread mentioned in one of the wedding songs:

> El hilo tropieza
> con el pedernal.
> Los montes azules
> lo dejan pasar.
> Corre, corre, corre,
> y al fin llegará
> a poner cuchillo
> y quitar el pan.

[29] Kurt Schindler, *Folk Music and Poetry of Spain and Portugal* (New York: Hispanic Institute in the United States, 1941), no. 702.

As the skein is unwound even further, the riddle of life is gradually clarified and resolved in the Niña's final song, which traces the end of the thread to the very room in which the Muchachas are unwinding it; the *madeja*'s hopeless dream of spinning a "cristal de papel" is dashed by the reality of mud-covered corpses:

> Corre, corre, corre,
> el hilo hasta aquí.
> Cubiertos de barro
> los siento venir.
> ¡Cuerpos estirados,
> paños de marfil!

The association in this song of the symbolic thread of life with the fact of two corpses shows how intimately Lorca's songs are related to actual events and how he raised circumstances of reality to a level of lyricism. One of the most striking features of *Bodas de sangre* is this intimate correspondence between fact and the poeticization of fact, and our full understanding and enjoyment of the play depend on our following Lorca's constant passage between one plane and the other. However superficially distinguishable they may be, dialogue, poems and songs are mutually dependent and mutually enriching; they underline, support and illuminate one another in the same way as the Madre, who belongs to this life, is defined and complemented by the Mendiga, who does not. The images of death Lorca put into the Mendiga's mouth — from the "cofres", "blancos hilos" and "cuerpos pesados" of her first speech (III, i) to the "sucia arena" of her last (III, ii) — relate her to the Madre: she voices and represents the Madre's obsession, and if the Madre at the end of the play is "tranquila", it is because the Mendiga has engineered the death which the Madre so feared and yet by her undying hatred did so much to bring about. The Madre and Mendiga, though they speak with two voices, are really one mind.

6. *Conclusion*

D OTTED throughout *Bodas de sangre* are a number of epi-
grammatic statements which, independent of what actually
happens in the play, encapsulate a vision of life that is deeply
pessimistic. The Madre's tersely expressed beliefs — "Mientras
una vive, lucha" and "Los varones son del viento" (II, ii) —
proclaim the pain of living and the certainty of dying as unequivocally as Leonardo's oracular conviction that

> La misma llama pequeña
> mata dos espigas juntas. (III, i)

In giving death a recognizable form and human dimensions in
the person of the Mendiga, Lorca shows how free it is to wander
unrecognized in our midst. "Doña Muerte" had already appeared in *Libro de poemas* in the poem 'Canción para la luna'
(I, p. 57). Her re-appearance in *Bodas de sangre* in the forest
and then in the house embodies in one figure Lorca's belief
that death can arrive at any place, at any time.

The victims claimed by death in *Bodas de sangre* and during
the events which preceded the play met violent ends; the hideously maimed Rafael is both a victim and a stunted survivor
of the violence which, dominating this tragedy, runs as a constant strain through Lorca's work and Lorca's mind. In his
stimulating book John Fraser maintains:

> To involve oneself with violence can indeed compel one
> into thought about oneself and man and society, some-
> times very painful and disconcerting thought. [30]

[30] *Violence in the Arts,* Illustrated paperback edition (Cambridge:
University Press, 1976), p. 110.

Throughout *Bodas de sangre* we are made aware of the threat posed by knives, and the Madre's relentless cursing of the weapons that ended the lives of her husband and son is justified by the Mendiga's graphically precise instruction to the Moon:

> Ilumina el chaleco y aparta los botones,
> que después las navajas ya saben el camino. (III, i)

This sense of menace is reinforced on another level by a series of matching images of pain and penetration, which represent the sufferings of the central characters, particularly in the scene of imminent death in the forest. Within minutes of each other the Novia and Leonardo exclaim: "¡Qué vidrios se me clavan en la lengua!" (III, i). Leonardo goes on to recall that

> Con alfileres de plata
> mi sangre se puso negra...

They are tormented not only from within by their own words and feelings, but from without by the breeze, which, according to the Luna, "va llegando duro, con doble filo" (III, i), and by the Moon itself, whose beams cleave the air like a knife:

> La luna deja un cuchillo
> abandonado en el aire,
> que siendo acecho de plomo
> quiere ser dolor de sangre. (III, i)

For Lorca violence is clearly a fact of life, a commonplace malady for which no antidote can be found. Certainly the bland, self-righteous entreaties of "Amor, amor, amor" and "paz, paz, paz" made by the Pope in 'Grito hacia Roma', in *Poeta en Nueva York,* are drowned by the metallic, explosive noises of murder and destruction irrupting in "el tirite de cuchillos y melones de dinamita" (I, p. 526). In the same poem Lorca visualized "un millón de carpinteros / que hacen ataúdes sin cruz" (I, p. 525). The crosses which we see or to which characters allude in *Bodas de sangre* are a mocking reminder of a religion that, powerless to prevent brutal murders, provides no comfort in adversity. The "cruz de grandes flores rosa"

Lorca placed in the Novia's cave promises as little hope and charity as the "cruz de ceniza" mentioned by the Suegra and the "cruz de amargas adelfas" mentioned by the Madre after the deaths of the two men (III, ii). In calling hurriedly in the closing moments of the play for "La cruz, la cruz", the Madre does what is expected of her; she observes a ritual which had been respected by the Madre in 'Canción de la madre del Amargo', in *Poema del cante jondo*, who also demanded the liturgical prayer:

> La cruz. No llorad ninguna.
> El Amargo está en la luna. (I, p. 241)

In *Bodas de sangre* the Mujeres' response to the Madre's command is instantaneous and automatic: they intone a short prayer:

> Dulces clavos,
> dulce cruz,
> dulce nombre
> de Jesús.

As they echo the brevity and rhythmic lilt of such traditional invocations as

> Cruz santa,
> Cruz bendita,
> Tú me salvas,
> Tú me guías, [31]

the mourning women show themselves to be prisoners of tradition, conditioned by upbringing to intone responses as mechanical as that of the Madre, who answers their prayer with the entreaty "Que la cruz ampare a muertos y vivos". The Madre says what she has to say because it is expected of her; her parrot-like statement cannot conceal the fact that the violent deaths of her son and Leonardo challenge the Christian doctrines of love and forgiveness represented by the cross. *Bodas*

[31] Rodríguez Marín, *Cantos populares españoles*, I, no. 1037.

Bibliographical Note

1. Alberich, José, 'El erotismo femenino en el teatro de García Lorca', *Papeles de Son Armadans*, XXXIX (1965), 8–36.
   An important article, with illuminating comments on *Bodas de sangre*.

2. Allen, Rupert Jr., 'A Symbological Commentary on *Blood Wedding*' in his *Psyche and Symbol in the Theater of Federico García Lorca* (Austin: Univ. of Texas Press, 1974), pp.161–211.
   A provocative commentary on the lullaby and the Moon's soliloquy.

3. Anderson, Reed, 'The Idea of Tragedy in García Lorca's *Bodas de sangre*', *Revista Hispánica Moderna*, XXXVIII (1974–75), 174–88.
   An attempt to explain the tragedy of *Bodas de sangre* as the rupture of relationships and family units.

4. Barnes, Peter, 'The Fusion of Poetry and Drama in *Blood Wedding*', *Modern Drama*, II (1958–60), 395–402.
   Some useful comments on colour and image patterns.

5. Correa, Gustavo, 'Bodas de sangre', in his *La poesia mítica de Federico García Lorca* (Madrid: Gredos, 1970), pp.82–116.
   A sound and wide-ranging essay.

6. Dickson, Ronald J., 'Archetypal Symbolism in Lorca's *Bodas de sangre*', *Literature and Psychology*, X (1960), 76–79.
   A Jungian analysis of the play.

7. Gaskell, Ronald, 'Theme and Form: Lorca's *Blood Wedding*', *Modern Drama*, V (1962–63), 431–39.
   Perceptive comments on imagery, rhythms and styles.

8. Goldfaden, Bruce M., '*Bodas de sangre* and *La dama del alba*', *Hispania*, XLIV (1961), 234–36.
   Brief but perceptive comments on the role of women.

9. González del Valle, Luis, '*Bodas de sangre* y sus elementos trágicos', *Archivum*, XXI (1971), 95–120.
   A diffuse treatment of tragic elements.

10. ——, 'Justicia poética en *Bodas de sangre*', *Romance Notes*, XIV (1972–73), 236–41.
    An attempt to show how poetic justice is brought into operation by the errors of the Madre and Novia.

11. Halliburton, Charles Lloyd, 'García Lorca, the Tragedian: An

Aristotelian Analysis of *Bodas de sangre*', *Revista de Estudios Hispánicos*, II (1968), 35–40.

    An attempt to show *Bodas de sangre* as a "complex" tragedy.

12. Jareño, Ernesto, '*El caballero de Olmedo*, García Lorca y Albert Camus', *Papeles de Son Armadans*, LVIII (1970), 219–42.

    Interesting observations about some possible sources of *Bodas de sangre*.

13. Martínez Nadal, Rafael, 'El caballo en la obra de García Lorca', in his *El público. Amor, teatro y caballos en la obra de Federico García Lorca* (Oxford: Dolphin, 1970), pp.193–233.

    A comprehensive survey.

14. Nonoyama, Minako, 'La función de los símbolos en *Pelléas et Mélisande* de Maeterlinkck, *Bodas de sangre* de Lorca y *Riders to the Sea* de Synge', *Revista de Estudios Hispánicos*, IX (1975), 81–98.

    A sensible consideration of the recurrence, rather than the function, of several symbols.

15. Palley, Julian, 'Archetypal Symbols in *Bodas de sangre*', *Hispania*, L (1967), 74–79.

    Sensible comments on a number of symbols.

16. Riley, Edward C., 'Sobre *Bodas de sangre*', *Clavileño*, 7 (enero-febrero 1951), 8–12.

    Important comments on honour and fate.

17. Smoot, Jean J., 'A Comparative Study of *Riders to the Sea* and *Bodas de sangre*', in her *A Comparison of Plays by John Millington Synge and Federico García Lorca: The Poets and Time* (Madrid: Porrúa Turanzas, 1978), pp.63–97.

    A detailed, but sometimes strained, comparison.

18. Timm, John T.H., 'Some Critical Observation on García Lorca's *Bodas de sangre*', *Revista de Estudios Hispánicos*, VII (1973), 255–88.

    Some sensible comments amid misreadings and naive interpretations.

19. Touster, Eva K., 'Thematic Patterns in Lorca's *Blood Wedding*', *Modern Drama*, VII (1964), 16–27.

    A good discussion of the play's major images.

20. Villegas, Juan, 'El leitmotiv del caballo en *Bodas de sangre*', *Hispanófila*, 29 (enero 1967), 21–36.

    A comprehensive analysis.

SUPPLEMENTARY BIBLIOGRAPHY

21. Aguilar Piñal, Francisco, 'La honra en el teatro de García Lorca', *Revista de Literatura*, 48. no.96 (July–Dec. 1986), 447–54.

22. Ajala, John D., 'Similarities between J.M. Synge's *Riders to the Sea* and Federico García Lorca's *Blood Wedding*', *College Language Association Journal*, 28 (1985), 314–25.

23. Albert-Galera, Josefina, 'La isotopía muerte como configuradora de *Bodas de sangre* de García Lorca', in Asociación Española de Semiótica, ed., *Investigaciones semióticas. II: Lo teatral y lo cotidiano* (Universidad de Oviedo, 1988), 53–67.

24. Alvarez-Altman, Grace, '*Blood Wedding*: A Literary Onomastic Interpretation', *García Lorca Review*, VIII (1980), 60–72.

25. ——, 'The Empty Nest Syndrome in García Lorca's Major Dramas', *García Lorca Review*, XI (1983), 149–59.

26. Anderson, Andrew A., 'García Lorca's *Bodas de sangre*: The Logic and Necessity of Act Three', *Hispanófila*, 30 (1987), no.90, 21–37.

27. ——, 'The Strategy of García Lorca's Dramatic Composition 1930–1936', *Romance Quarterly*, 33 (1986), 211–29.

28. Arce, Carlos de, *El crimen de Níjar* (Calella: Seuba Ediciones, 1988).

29. Balboa-Echevarría, Miriam, 'Nanas, prisión y deseo en *Bodas de sangre*', *Confluencia*, 9 (Spring 1994), 98–108.

30. Béjel, Emilio, 'Las funciones dramáticas de *Bodas de sangre*', *Hispanófila*, 27 (1984), no.80, 87–94.

31. Burton, Julianne, 'The Greatest Punishment: Female and Male in Lorca's Tragedies', in Beth Miller, ed., *Women in Hispanic Literature: Icons and Fallen Idols* (Berkeley: University of California Press, 1983), pp.259–79.

32. Colecchia, Francesca, 'The Religious Ambience in the Trilogy: A Definition', *García Lorca Review*, X (1982), 24–42.

33. Doménech, Ricardo, 'Sobre la "nana del caballo" en *Bodas de sangre*', *Trece de Nieve*, 2nd series, no.1–2 (December 1976), 202–09.

34. ——, 'Realidad misterio: Notas sobre el espacio escénico en *Bodas de sangre, Yerma* y *La casa de Bernarda Alba*', *Cuadernos Hispanoamericanos*, no.433–34 (July–August 1986), 293–310.

35. Elizalde, Ignacio, 'La metáfora en la estructura poética de *Bodas de sangre*', in Miguel Angel Garrido Gallardo, ed., *Crítica semiológica de textos literarios hispánicos* (Madrid: Consejo Superior de Investigaciones Científicas, 1986), pp.665–78.

36. Feal, Carlos, 'El sacrificio de la hombría en *Bodas de sangre*', *Modern Language Notes*, 99 (1984), 270–87; reprinted in *Lorca: tragedia y mito*, Ottawa Hispanic Studies 4 (Ottawa: Dovehouse Editions, 1989), pp.41–62.

37. Feito, Francisco E., 'Synge y Lorca: de *Riders to the Sea* a *Bodas de sangre*', *García Lorca Review*, IX (1981), 144–52.

38. García, María J., 'Realidad y ficción en *Bodas de sangre*', *Vida Hispánica*, 1 (1990), 28–30.

39. Greenfield, Sumner, 'Lorca's Tragedies: Practice Without Theory', *Siglo XX/20th Century*, 4 (1986–1987), 1–5.

40. Hernández, Mario, 'Cronología de *Bodas de sangre* (1928–1938)', in Piero Menarini, ed., *Lorca* (Bologna: Atesa, 1987), pp.43–63.

41. Herrero, Javier, 'The Dance of Death: The Moon as Hunter', in Ramón Fernández Rubio, ed., *Selected Proceedings of the 35th Annual Mountain Interstate Foreign Language Conference* (Greenville, South Carolina: Furman University, 1987), pp.193–209.

42. Klein, Dennis A., *Blood Wedding, Yerma and The House of Bernarda Alba: García Lorca's Tragic Trilogy* (Boston: Twayne, 1991).

43. López, Daniel, '*Bodas de sangre* and *La dama del alba*: Compared and Contrasted', *Revista de Estudios Hispánicos*, 15 (1981), 407–23.

44. Loughran, David K., 'Imagery of Nature and its Function in Lorca's Poetic Drama: "Reyerta" and *Bodas de sangre*', in Joseph W. Zdenek, ed., *The World of Nature in the Works of Federico García Lorca* (Winthrop College: Winthrop Studies on Major Modern Writers, 1980), pp.55–61.

45. McDermott, Patricia, 'Death as a Way of Life: Lorca's Dramatic Subversion of Orthodoxy', in Margaret Rees, ed., *Leeds Papers on Hispanic Drama* (Leeds: Trinity and All Saints College, 1991), pp.125–52.

46. Macmillan, Terence, 'Federico García Lorca's Critique of Marriage in *Bodas de sangre*', *Neophilologus*, 77 (1993), 61–73.

47. Macri, Oreste, 'Da un "follito" per *Nozze di sangue*', *Quaderni Ibero-Americani*, 65–66 (1989), 2–5.

48. Maurer, Christopher, 'Bach and *Bodas de sangre*', in M. Durán and Francesca Colecchia, eds., *Lorca's Legacy: Essays on Lorca's Life, Poetry, and Theatre* (Peter Lang, 1991), pp.103–14.

49. Miller, Norman C., 'Lullaby, Wedding Song and Funeral Chant in García Lorca's *Bodas de sangre*', *Gestos: Teoría y práctica del teatro hispánico*, 3 (1988), no.5, 41–51.

50. Ortega, José, 'Conciencia social en los tres dramas rurales de García Lorca', *García Lorca Review*, IX (1981), 64–90.

51. Ralph, Wendy L., 'Lorca/Gades/Saura: Modes of Representation in *Bodas de sangre*', *Anales de Literatura Española Contemporánea*, 11 (1986), 193–204.

52. Romero, Hector R., 'El protagonista y la estructura dramática: Dos elementos inseparables en la dimensión trágica de *Bodas de sangre*', *Mester*, 15 (1986), 38–46.

53. ——, 'Hacia un concepto dualista sobre el personaje trágico en *Bodas de sangre*', *García Lorca Review*, X (1982), 50–60.

54. Smoot, Jeanne J., 'The Living Text in the Drama of John Millington Synge and Federico García Lorca', in Anna Balakian et al, ed.,

Proceedings of the Xth Congress of the International Comparative Literature Association (New York: 1982), Vol.I, pp.38–42.

55. Soufas, C. Christopher, 'Interpretation in/of *Bodas de sangre*', *García Lorca Review*, XI (1983), 53–74.

56. ——, '*Bodas de sangre* and the Problematics of Representation', *Revista de Estudios Hispánicos*, 21 (1987), 29–48.

57. Stainton, Leslie, 'A Concept of Land: José Luis Gómez, Lorca, and *Bodas de sangre*', *Anales de Literatura Española Contemporánea*, 11 (1986), 205–13.

58. Tinnell, Roger, 'La música perdida de *Bodas de sangre*', *ABC Cultural*, 6 August 1993, p.34.

59. Vermeylen, A., 'Du fait divers à la tragédie: A propos de *Noces de sang* de García Lorca', *Les Lettres Romanes*, 39 (1985), 125–38.

60. Walsh, John K., 'A Genesis for García Lorca's *Bodas de sangre*', *Hispania*, 72 (1991), 255–61.

CRITICAL GUIDES TO SPANISH TEXTS

Edited by
J.E. Varey, A.D. Deyermond & C. Davies

CRITICAL GUIDES TO SPANISH TEXTS

Edited by
J.E. Varey, A.D. Deyermond & C. Davies